Reflections

on

Yogasūtra-s of Patañjali

T. K. V. Desikachar

Published by

Krishnamacharya Yoga Mandiram

31, 4th Cross Street, R K Nagar, Chennai - 600028, India

Revised Edition - March 2003 / Reprinted - December 2003
ISBN: 81-87847-20-4
Paperback Edition - For Sale in India Only

This book was previously published by Affiliated East-West Press Pvt.Ltd. as "*Patañjali's Yoga Sūtra-s* - **An Introduction**" - ISBN : 81-85095-61-2. This book is a revised and updated edition of the first book with useful inclusions that form Parts II and III.

English Translation and Commentary: T K V Desikachar

Project Editor : Kausthub Desikachar

Edited by : Nrithya Jagannathan

Layout Design : T Raman Pillai

Cover Design : Kausthub Desikachar

Printed by: Quadra Press Ltd., Nandanam, Chennai - 35.

Contents

Introduction

India has been the birthplace of numerous ancient philosophies, which are timeless in their appeal and relevance. Of all these philosophies which originated over a span of around two thousand years, the ancient discipline of Yoga, is one that enjoys tremendous popularity the world over. The inherent simplicity and practicality of the teachings of Yoga, have made Yoga a household concept to millions of people in every corner of the world.

Today, as the importance of Yoga in every aspect of life is realized, more students and practitioners of Yoga are looking deeper into the philosophical basis of Yoga. There are questions galore - What is the origin of Yoga? What is its final reference? Does it comprise just body practices, as is popularly perceived – thanks to the popularity of *āsana*, one of its many tools? How can Yoga influence life, attitudes and well being? As we seek the answers to these and more queries, the search invariably leads us to the very heart of Yoga – the *Yoga Sūtra-s* of *Patañjali*.

Believed to be at least two thousand years old, this brief, yet precise text has been acknowledged as the ultimate source of reference on Yoga. In fact, according to the *yogi-s* of the past, "if a concept is mentioned in the *Yoga Sūtra-s*, it is very important to take note of it; while if a concept is not mentioned in this masterpiece, then it either has nothing to do with Yoga or is irrelevant". Such was the importance given to this timeless classic.

The *Yoga Sūtra-s* constitute the basis and reference for the six schools of Indian philosophy which are derived from the *Veda-s*. The *Veda-s* are a huge compilation of sacred hymns that were heard by different sages when they were in meditation. The ancient masters compiled all these hymns, which in totality represented a huge body of wisdom that discussed all issues relating to daily life. Believed to be the voice of God, these hymns were revered as the ultimate authority for any question. So, when people had a conflict of any sort, they would turn to the *Veda-s* for guidance.

However, being inspirational in nature, the compilation was not very well organized. Also, the language of the *Veda-s* was archaic and over time, it became increasingly difficult for people to comprehend and interpret accurately, the message of the *Veda-s*. This led to confused and incorrect interpretations that consequently did more harm than good.

It was at this time that six different masters, who were probably contemporaries (but one can never be sure) evolved the six schools of Indian philosophy. Each of these schools was based on concepts from the *Veda-s* and contained messages that would help alleviate suffering. All these schools of thought were oriented towards the reduction of suffering, but they prescribed different paths towards this goal. Since these schools of thought branched off from the *Veda-s*, they are known as "*Vaidika Darśana-s*" and can thus be considered children of the same mother. However, in spite of certain similarities, like many children born of the same parents, they are quite different in their essential teachings.

This indicates the boundless wisdom of the *Veda-s*, and hence must be understood precisely. The *Veda-s* are not only a collection of works that represent a particular philosophy. Rather, they have associations with many issues that concern our daily lives and provide different approaches to deal with these issues. What is significant is that the *Veda-s* cannot be identified solely with Hinduism. This is because, among the six schools that are derived from the *Veda-s*, only three recognized the existence of a supreme being whom we may call God. The philosophies that the *Veda-s* embody are beyond the confines of religion.

These three schools of thought are *Vedānta*, *Mīmāmsa* and Yoga. Of these, only *Vedānta* and *Mīmāmsa* stress on belief in God. In the school of Yoga, *Patañjali* perceives God as a choice. Yoga is thus, open even to people who do not believe in the concept of God. It is because Yoga does not insist on conformity to any particular religious faith, that it holds a universal appeal

Although all the schools of philosophy strive to achieve the same goal – freedom from suffering, Yoga recognizes the existence of the human mind and acknowledges its role in our day to day functioning. According to *Patañjali,* the mind is both the source of and solution to our problems. If the mind is agitated, distracted or conditioned by habit, then perception may be inaccurate, landing us in trouble. However, if the same mind is disciplined, focused and free from habits, perception is more accurate and therefore our actions based on this perception will not cause suffering. This is the crux of *Patañjali's* philosophy of Yoga.

It is ironical that the credit for analyzing the human mind and its functioning goes to an Austrian psychologist who probably lived in the last century. A careful study of the *Yoga Sūtra-s* will reveal *Patañjali's* profound understanding of the human mind. *Patañjali* makes this message very clear early in the text. His approach is that each mind is different and hence, different tools are needed to reduce the mental agitation of different people. In his extraordinary treatment, *Patañjali* respects every individual as a unique being, different not just at the physical level but also in terms of energy and the mental, emotional and spiritual aspects of existence. This is why he suggests a wide variety of tools to chose from, in order to make the mind calmer, more focused and disciplined. This is why he even suggests that the concept of God be a matter of individual choice. For those who believe in God, the concept of God may be useful as an anchor with which to find peace, whereas for those of us who do not believe in God, this might not work. The liberty with which *Patañjali* presents the pursuit of a religion purely as a conscious choice unique to the individual, highlights the sensitivity of his analysis of the human mind.

Presented in four chapters the *Yoga Sūtra-s* are a compilation of 195 aphorisms that cover the entire philosophical wisdom of Yoga.

The first chapter presents the goal of Yoga, which is to reach a state of mind that is full of attention and devoid of distraction. The second chapter gives us insights into some of the practical tools of Yoga which help us attain this state. The third and fourth chapters present the immense potentials of the human mind, facilitated by the state of Yoga. The third chapter elaborates on the powers that we may gain through the state of Yoga, simultaneously warning us that these powers may themselves act as obstacles on the path to freedom from suffering. The fourth chapter takes us beyond these powers and expounds on the role of this state of mind brought about by Yoga, in our own transformation and progress towards freedom from suffering.

While talking about the philosophy of Yoga, it is very important for us to remember that Yoga is not restricted to the physical body as is commonly misunderstood today. Yoga goes beyond the physical, in that it deals with the human mind. *Patañjali* presents the practice of body postures only as a means of bringing about a calmer and more focused state of mind. Like all the other tools he prescribes, if this practice of postures does not help us reach a more calmer and attentive state of mind, then it is useless. This is something we must remember, because the practice of *āsana-s* should not be likened to mere acrobatics. These practices play a role in influencing the mind and must therefore, be based on the principles that will help us achieve this.

Interpretation of the *Yoga Sūtra-s* of *Patañjali* is an important issue. This is because this text has been presented in Sanskrit, a language that is both profound and rich. The aphorismatic style also complicates interpretation, because the *Sūtra-s* primarily comprise certain phrases that only give direction. It is up to the teacher to unravel the many layers of meaning contained in the *Sūtra-s*. Mere knowledge of Sanskrit or the ability to refer a dictionary is not enough to understand and interpret this great teaching. This is because Sanskrit words have multiple meanings and choice of one particular interpretation depends not only on the root meaning of the word but also on the context in which it has been used. For example if one looked up a Sanskrit dictionary to refer the word "*āsana*", one of many meanings would be "chair" or "seat", but this does not fit into the context of the *Yoga Sūtra-s*. Obviously *Patañjali* is not talking about a chair or a seat when he discusses *āsana* as one of the eight limbs of Yoga. It is, hence, important to have a competent teacher, who not only has a thorough understanding of the language but has also experienced the philosophy of Yoga through his/her own study and practice.

We are fortunate to have this translation by one such eminent master, T K V Desikachar who is regarded as one of the great authorities on Yoga. Son and student of legendary master T Krishnamacharya, Desikachar studied with his father for over three decades. It is with the wisdom born of so many years of study, that he shares through this very simple translation ideal for anyone who is interested in the philosophy of Yoga, the message contained in the *Yoga Sūtra-s* of *Patañjali*.

Enjoy this journey.

Kausthub Desikachar,
Krishnamacharya Yoga Mandiram

Pronunciation Guide

Guttural (pronounced from the throat)

Vowels	a	as in but
	ā	as in father
Plain	k	as in kin
	g	as in good
Aspirate	kh	as in sinkhole
	gh	as in leghorn
	h	as in hand
Nasal	ṅ	as in encore

Palatal (pronounced from the palate)

Vowels	i	as in tin
	ī	as in teeth
Plain	c	as in church
	j	as in judge
Aspirate	ch	as in coachhorse
	jh	as in hedgehog
Semi-vowel	y	as in you
Sibilant	ś	as in sure

Retroflex (pronounced with the tip of the tongue curled up)

Vowel	ṛ	as in sab<u>r</u>e
Plain	ṭ	as in car<u>t</u>
	ḍ	as in ar<u>d</u>ent
Aspirate	ṭh	as in car<u>th</u>orse
	ḍh	as in for<u>dh</u>am
Nasal	ṇ	as in frie<u>n</u>d
Semi-vowel	r	as in <u>r</u>ib
Sibilant	ṣ	as in hu<u>sh</u>

Dental (pronounced with the tip of the tongue against upper teeth)

Vowel	ḷ	as in ab<u>l</u>e
Plain	t	as in <u>th</u>eatre
	d	as in <u>th</u>ey
Aspirate	th	as in wi<u>thh</u>eld
	dh	as in bu<u>ddh</u>a
Nasal	n	as in boo<u>n</u>
Semi-vowel	l	as in <u>l</u>ip
Sibilant	s	as in <u>s</u>un

Labial (pronounced with the lips)

Vowels	u	as in bull
	ū	as in rule
Plain	p	as in pat
	b	as in bee
Aspirate	ph	as in uphill
	bh	as in abhor
Nasal	m	as in man

Guttural and Palatal

Vowels	e	as in prey
	ai	as in aisle

Guttural and Labial

Vowels	o	as in go
	au	as in cow

Dental and Labial

Semi-vowel	v	as in van

Nasal

ṁ or ṅ makes the preceding vowel nasal

Aspirate

ḥ makes the preceding vowel aspirate

How to Use this Book

Please use this guide as an indicator of how to use this book

> ***Sūtra I.2*** → 1
>
> योगश्चित्तवृत्तिनिरोधः । → 2
>
> *yogaścittavṛttinirodhaḥ* → 3
>
> What is Yoga? It is a word that has many interpretations and connotations. *Patañjali* defines his understanding of the word. → 4
>
> *Yoga is the ability to direct the mind exclusively towards an object and sustain focus in that direction without any distractions.* → 5
>
> The object can be a concrete one, either external to ourselves or part of ourselves. It can be an area of interest, a concept or something beyond the level of the senses, such as God. → 4

1 - This represents the chapter followed by the *sūtra* number

2 - The actual *sūtra* in Sanskrit

3 - Transliteration of the *sūtra*

4 - T K V Desikachar's Commentary and thoughts

5 - English Translation of the verse by T K V Desikachar *

* The translation of the *sūtra-s* is indicated through the use of Italics, to be distinguished from T K V Desikachar's commentary which is given in normal font

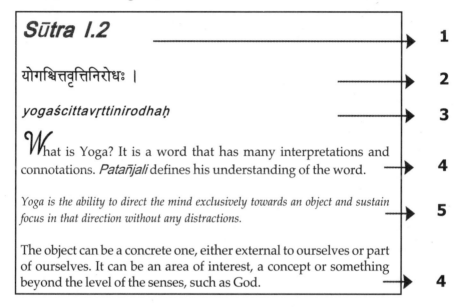

Part - I

Yoga Sūtra-s
Text, Transliteration, Translation & Commentary

Chapter 1

समाधिपादः
Samādhipādaḥ

The *sūtra-s* of *Patañjali* are presented in four chapters. The first chapter is called *Samādhipādaḥ* (the chapter on *samādhi*). This chapter defines Yoga and its characteristics. It further discusses the problems encountered in reaching the state of Yoga and how these problems can be handled.

I.1

अथ योगानुशासनम् ।

atha yogānuśāsanam

The first *sūtra* introduces the subject matter, as the oral tradition requires. In the convention of ancient Sanskrit literature, the first word, *atha*, carries the connotation of a prayer, both for an auspicious beginning and a successful conclusion to the work which follows.

Here begins the authoritative instruction on Yoga.

Patañjali indicates that, while the subject matter is of ancient origin and he is not the source, he has studied and practiced it to an appropriate depth under his own teacher and is now competent to share his understanding with his disciples. His style will be in a manner suitable for them to transmit this knowledge in turn to their disciples through traditional oral methods.

I.2

योगश्चित्तवृत्तिनिरोधः ।

yogaścittavṛttinirodhaḥ

What is Yoga? It is a word that has many interpretations and connotations. *Patañjali* defines his understanding of the word.

Yoga is the ability to direct the mind exclusively towards an object and sustain focus in that direction without any distractions.

The object can be a concrete one, either external to ourselves or part of ourselves. It can be an area of interest, a concept or something beyond the level of the senses, such as God.

I.3

तदा द्रष्टुः स्वरूपेऽवस्थानम् ।

tadā draṣṭuḥ svarūpe'vāsthānam

Then, the ability to understand the object fully and correctly is apparent.

In the state of Yoga, the different preconceptions and products of the imagination that can prevent or distort understanding are controlled, reduced or eliminated. The tendency to be closed to fresh comprehension or the inability to comprehend are overcome.

I.4

वृत्तिसारूप्यमितरत्र ।

vṛttisārūpyamitaratra

In the absence of the state of mind called Yoga

The ability to understand the object is simply replaced by the mind's conception of that object or by a total lack of comprehension.

A disturbed mind can rarely focus on a single direction. If it ever does, comprehension of the object will be faulty.

I.5

वृत्तयः पञ्चतय्यः क्लिष्टाक्लिष्टाः ।

vṛttayaḥ pañcatayyaḥ kliṣṭākliṣṭāḥ

What is the mind? *Patañjali* defines the mind as a composite of the activities that occupy it. It cannot be perceived except in terms of these activities.

There are five activities of the mind. Each of these can be beneficial and each can cause problems.

Whether these activities are beneficial or will create problems cannot be seen immediately. Time alone will confirm their effects.

I.6

प्रमाणविपर्ययविकल्पनिद्रास्मृतयः ।

pramāṇaviparyayavikalpanidrāsmṛtayaḥ

The five activities are comprehension, misapprehension, imagination, deep sleep and memory.

Each mental activity has its own characteristics and although not always apparent, these can be individually recognized. Their dominance and effects on our behaviour and attitudes combine to make up our personalities.

I.7

प्रत्यक्षानुमानागमाः प्रमाणानि ।

pratyakṣānumānāgamāḥ pramāṇāni

The activities are defined individually.

Comprehension is based on direct observation of the object, inference and reference to reliable authorities.

The mind can register an object directly through the senses. When the information available is inadequate or incomplete, for sensual perception, other faculties such as logic and memory may enable a more complete comprehension of the object to be inferred. When no direct comprehension is possible, reference to reliable authorities, such as written texts or a trusted individual, can enable comprehension indirectly.

Thus do we understand places, people or concepts outside our direct experiences. Comprehension in the state of Yoga, is different from comprehension at other times. It is closer to the true nature of the object.

I.8

विपर्ययो मिथ्याज्ञानमतद्रूपप्रतिष्ठम् ।

viparyayo mithyājñānamatadrūpapratiṣṭham

Misapprehension is that comprehension which is taken to be correct until more favorable conditions reveal the actual nature of the object.

This is considered to be the most frequent activity of the mind. Misapprehension may occur through faulty observation or the misinterpretation of what is seen. It is caused due to our inability to understand in depth what we see, often as a result of past experiences and conditioning. The error may be recognized later or never at all. The aim of Yoga practice is to recognize and control the causes of misapprehension (*Patañjali* explores this in chapter two).

I.9

शब्दज्ञानानुपाती वस्तुशून्यो विकल्पः ।

śabdajñānānupātī vastuśūnyo vikalpaḥ

Imagination is the comprehension of an object based only on words and expressions, even though the object is absent.

Imagination happens in the absence of any direct perception. Reference to the meaning, connotations or implications of descriptive words guides imagination towards comprehension. It may be further helped if the words are used poetically or oratorically. It can also arise through other means such as dreams, feelings and emotions. Past experiences, stored as memory, often contribute to this mental activity.

I.10

अभावप्रत्ययालम्बना तमोवृत्तिर्निद्रा ।

abhāvapratyayālambanā tamovṛttirnidrā

Deep sleep is when the mind is overcome with heaviness and no other activities are present.

Sleep is a common activity for the mind and there is a certin time for it. But the heaviness can also occur due to boredom or exhaustion, resulting in sleep. Sleep is a regular condition for all living beings.

I.11

अनुभूतविषयासंप्रमोषः स्मृतिः ।

anubhūtaviṣayāsaṁpramoṣaḥ smṛtiḥ

Memory is the mental retention of a conscious experience.

All conscious experiences leave an impression on the individual and are stored as memory. It is not possible to tell if a memory is true, false, incomplete or imaginary.

All and each of these activities of the mind confirm the existence of the mind. They are interrelated and complex, so that each one, except perhaps sleep, should be considered as a matrix or genus of activity rather than as a distinct entity with exclusive and limited characteristics. Each can, at different times and in diferent circumstances, be both beneficial and harmful. Their effects may be direct and immediate or they may be indirect as a later consequence of their manifestation.

I.12

अभ्यासवैराग्याभ्यां तन्निरोधः ।

abhyāsavairāgyābhyāṁ tannirodhaḥ

How do we arrive at the state of Yoga? What should we do and what should we not do?

The mind can reach the state of Yoga through practice and detachment.

I.13

तत्र स्थितौ यत्नोऽभ्यासः ।

tatra sthitau yatno'bhyāsaḥ

What are the essential features of this practice and detachment? Even though the techniques involved are not specified here, the following two *sūtra-s* indicate their qualities.

Practice is basically the correct effort required to move towards, reach and maintain the state of Yoga (See I –2).

The practices chosen must be learned correctly from and guided by a competent teacher who understands the personal and social traits of the student. If the appropriate practice for a particular student is not provided and followed, there can be little hope of achieving success.

I.14

स तु दीर्घकालनैरन्तर्यसत्कारादरासेवितो दृढभूमिः ।

sa tu dīrghakālanairantaryasatkārādarāsevito dṛḍhabhūmiḥ

It is only when the correct practice is followed for a long time, without interruptions, and with a positive attitude and eagerness, that it can succeed.

There will always be a tendency to start practice with enthusiasm and energy, and a desire for immediate results. But, the continuing pressures of everyday life and the enormous resistance of the mind encourage us to succumb to human weaknesses. All this is understandable. We all have these tendencies. This *sūtra* emphasizes the need to approach practice soberly with a positive, self disciplined attitude and with a long term view towards eventual success.

I.15

दृष्टानुश्रविकविषयवितृष्णस्य वशीकारसंज्ञावैराग्यम् ।

dṛṣṭānuśravikaviṣayavitṛṣṇasya vaśīkārasaṁjñāvairāgyam

As we develop our practice along the correct lines, we find that our ability to discipline ourselves and reject intrusive influences grows. Eventually we may reach a state of detachment when

At the highest level there is an absence of any cravings, either for the fulfilment of the senses or for extraordinary experiences.

Practice gives benefits such as physical strength, dexterity, heightened awareness and sensitivity. There may also be the temptation to use our new skills to prove our higher state. But, these are incidental benefits and diversionary temptations, and if we place too much importance on them, we are in danger of losing sight of the path to the state of Yoga.

I.16

तत्परं पुरुषख्यातेर्गुणवैतृष्ण्यम् ।

tatparaṁ puruṣakhyāterguṇavaitṛṣṇyam

Further,

When an individual has achieved complete understanding of his true self, he will no longer be disturbed by the distracting influences within and around him.

Detachment develops with self understanding. The inevitable desires for diversion cannot be suppressed, for if they are, they will surely surface again later.

I.17

वितर्कविचारानन्दास्मितारूपानुगमात्संप्रज्ञातः ।

vitarkavicārānandāsmitārupānugamātsaṁprajñātaḥ

Then the object is gradually understood in totality. At first this understanding is at a more superficial level. In time, comprehension becomes deeper. And finally it is total. There is pure joy in reaching such a depth of understanding. For then, the individual is so much in unity with the object that he is oblivious to his surroundings.

Such a level of perception of the nature of the object is only possible in the state of yoga. Frequently we are able to understand the superficial and more obvious elements. But comprehension is incomplete until we have achieved perception at the deepest level without any errors.

I.18

विरामप्रत्ययाभ्यासपूर्वः संस्कारशेषोऽन्यः ।

virāmapratyayābhyāsapūrvaḥ saṁskāraśeṣo'nyaḥ

When the mind rises to the state of Yoga and remains so

The usual mental disturbances are absent. However, memories of the past continue.

Then, perception is immediate, not gradual. The memories remain to help us live in the day to day world, but do not create distractions.

I.19

भवप्रत्ययो विदेहप्रकृतिलयानाम् ।

bhavapratyayo videhaprakṛtilayānām

Inevitably, because of the many millions who share the world with us,

There will be some who are born in a state of Yoga. They need not practice or discipline themselves.

But, these are rare persons who cannot and should not be emulated. Indeed, some may succumb to wordly influences and lose their superior qualities.

I.20

श्रद्धावीर्यस्मृतिसमाधिप्रज्ञापूर्वक इतरेषाम् ।

śraddhāvīryasmṛtisamādhiprajñāpūrvaka itareṣām

But, what about the rest of us? Is there really a chance of achieving this state of Yoga?

Through faith, which will give sufficient energy to achieve success against all odds, direction will be maintained. The realization of the goal of Yoga is a matter of time.

The goal is the ability to direct the mind towards an object without any distraction, resulting in time, in a clear and correct understanding of that object.

Faith is the unshakeable conviction that we can arrive at a goal. We must not be complacent about success or discouraged by failure. We must work hard and steadily inspite of all distractions, whether good or bad.

I.21

तीव्रसंवेगानामासन्नः ।

tīvrasaṁvegānāmāsannaḥ

The more intense the faith and effort, the closer the goal.

I.22

मृदुमध्याधिमात्रत्वात्ततोऽपि विशेषः ।

mṛdumadhyādhimātratvāttato'pi viśeṣaḥ

Do we and can we all have the same degree of faith?

Inevitably, the depth of faith varies with different individuals and at different times with the same individual. The results will reflect these variations.

Such variations are a part of the human psyche. They are a product of the individual's cultural background and capabilities.

I.23

ईश्वरप्रणिधानाद्वा ।

īśvarapraṇidhānādvā

Patañjali recognizes that attempts to bring the mind to the state of Yoga are fraught with obstacles which vary in potency. But, for those who have either an inborn faith in God or are able to develop it over the years

Offering regular prayers to God with a feeling of submission to His power, surely enables the state of Yoga to be achieved.

In the following *sūtra-s*, *Patañjali* gives his definition of God.

I.24

क्लेशकर्मविपाकाशयैरपरामृष्टः पुरुषविशेष ईश्वरः ।

kleśakarmavipākāśayairaparāmṛṣṭaḥ puruṣaviśeṣa īśvaraḥ

God is the Supreme Being whose actions are never based on misapprehension.

I.25

तत्र निरतिशयं सर्वज्ञबीजम् ।

tatra niratiśayaṁ sarvajñabījam

How can God be so extraordinary?

He knows everything there is to be known.

His comprehension is beyond any human comparisons.

I.26

स एष पूर्वेषामपि गुरुः कालेनानवच्छेदात् ।

sa eṣa pūrveṣāmapi guruḥ kālenānavacchedāt

Is God, according to *Patañjali,* timebound or timeless?

God is eternal. In fact, He is the ultimate Teacher. He is the Source of guidance for all teachers, past, present and future.

I.27

तस्य वाचकः प्रणवः ।

tasya vācakaḥ praṇavaḥ

How should we refer to God? How should we address Him?

In the way most appropriate to the qualities of God.

In different cultures and different religions, different words are used to describe God and His qualities. It is more important that we refer to God with the greatest respect and without any conflicts. In this, a teacher can be of tremendous help.

I.28

तज्जपस्तदर्थभावनम् ।

tajjapastadarthabhāvanam

How do we relate to God?

In order to relate to God, it is necessary to regularly address Him properly and reflect on His qualities.

Patañjali suggests that it is necessary to reflect constantly on the qualities of God. This might be aided by the repeated recitation of His name along with prayer and contemplation. But mechanical repetition and prayer are worthless. This must be accompanied by conscious thought and consideration, and done with profound respect.

I.29

ततः प्रत्यक्चेतनाधिगमोऽप्यन्तरायाभावश्च ।

tataḥ pratyakcetanādhigamo'pyantarāyābhāvaśca

For those who have faith in God, such reflections will inevitably be beneficial.

The individual will in time perceive his true nature. He will not be disturbed by any interruptions that may arise in his journey to the state of Yoga.

I.30

व्याधिस्त्यानसंशयप्रमादालस्याविरति
भ्रान्तिदर्शनालब्धभूमिकत्वानवस्थितत्वानि
चित्तविक्षेपास्तेऽन्तरायाः ।

vyādhistyānasaṁśayapramādālasyāvirati bhrāntidarśanālabdhabhūmikatvānavasthitatvāni cittavikṣepāste'ntarāyāḥ

What, if any, are the interruptions?

There are nine types of interruptions to developing mental clarity. These are illness, mental stagnation, doubt, lack of foresight, fatigue, over indulgence, illusions about one's true state of mind, lack of perseverance and regression. These factors are obstacles to mental clarity because they create mental disurbances and encourage distractions.

The more vulnerable we are to these interruptions, the more difficult it is to reach a state of Yoga.

I.31

दुःखदौर्मनस्याङ्गमेजयत्वश्वासप्रश्वासा विक्षेपसहभुवः ।

duḥkhadaurmanasyāṅgamejayatvaśvāsapraśvāsā vikṣepasahabhuvaḥ

Can we tell when these interruptions are having an effect and taking root?

All these interruptions produce one or more of the following symptoms- mental discomfort, negative thinking, inability to be at ease in different body postures and difficulty in controlling one's breath.

Any of these symptoms can have further consequences. The following eight *sūtra-s* give some suggestions for controlling these interruptions and their symptoms. These suggestions are useful both for those with great faith in God and for atheists.

I.32

तत्प्रतिषेधार्थमेकतत्त्वाभ्यासः ।

tatpratiṣedhārthamekatattvābhyāsaḥ

If one can select an appropriate means to steady the mind and practice this, whatever the provocations, the interruptions cannot take root.

I.33

मैत्रीकरुणामुदितोपेक्षाणां सुखदुःखपुण्यापुण्यविषयाणां
भावनातश्चित्तप्रसादनम् ।

maitrīkaruṇāmuditopekṣāṇāṁ
sukhaduḥkhapuṇyāpuṇyaviṣayāṇāṁ
bhāvanātaścittaprasādanam

In daily life, we see around us people who are happier than we are and people who are less happy. Some may be doing things worthy of praise and others may be causing problems. Whatever be our usual attitudes towards such people and their actions, if we can be happy for those who are happier than ourselves, compassionate towards those who are not as happy, pleased with those whose activities are praiseworthy and remain undisturbed by the errors of others, our minds will be very tranquil.

I.34

प्रच्छर्दनविधारणाभ्यां वा प्राणस्य ।

pracchardanavidhāraṇābhyāṁ vā prāṇasya

When we find interruptions or the symptoms of interruptions

The practice of breathing exercises involving extended exhalation might be helpful.

These breathing techniques, however, must be correctly taught and guided.

I.35

विषयवती वा प्रवृत्तिरुत्पन्ना मनसः स्थितिनिबन्धिनी ।

viṣayavatī vā pravṛttirutpannā manasaḥ sthitinibandhinī

The role of senses, such as sight and hearing, in providing information to the mind is significant. These senses are the doors of perception and we are often their slaves. But, can we not examine what is even more powerful in us than our senses? Can we not make them sharper and at our disposal?

By regular enquiry into the role of the senses we can reduce mental distortions.

I.36

विशोका वा ज्योतिष्मती ।

viśokā vā jyotiṣmatī

One of the great mysteries of life is life itself.

When we enquire into what life is and what keeps us alive, we may find some solace for our mental distractions

Consideration of things greater than our individual selves helps us put ourselves in perspective.

I.37

वीतरागविषयं वा चित्तम् ।

vītarāgaviṣayaṁ vā cittam

When we are confronted with problems, the counsel of someone who has mastered similar problems can be a great help.

Such counsel can come directly from a living person or from the study of someone alive or dead.

I.38

स्वप्ननिद्राज्ञानालम्बनं वा ।

svapnanidrājñānālambanaṁ vā

When we believe we know a lot, we may become arrogant. The consequences can be disturbing. In fact, even the most ordinary, everyday occurrences are not always clear to us.

Enquiry into dreams and sleep and our experiences during or around these states can help to clarify some of our problems.

How refreshing it is after a good night's sleep! How disturbing a bad dream can be!

I.39

यथाभिमतध्यानाद्वा ।

yathābhimatadhyānādvā

Any enquiry of interest can calm the mind.

Sometimes the most simple objects of enquiry, such as the first cry of an infant, can help relieve mental disturbances. Sometimes complex enquiries should not replace the main goal, which remains to change our state of mind gradually from distraction to direction.

I – 40

परमाणुपरममहत्त्वान्तोऽस्य वशीकारः ।

paramāṇuparamamahattvānto'sya vaśīkāraḥ

What are the consequences of developing this state of Yoga?

When one reaches this state, nothing is beyond comprehension. The mind can follow and help in the understanding of the simple and the complex, the infinite and the infinitesimal, the perceptible and the imperceptible.

The actual process of this comprehension is explained below.

I.41

क्षीणवृत्तेरभिजातस्येव मणेर्ग्रहीतृग्रहणग्राह्येषु
तत्स्थतदञ्जनता समापत्तिः ।

kṣīṇavṛtterabhijātasyeva maṇergrahītṛgrahaṇagrāhyeṣu tatsthatadañjanatā samāpattiḥ

When the mind is free from distraction, it is possible for all the mental processes to be involved in the object of enquiry. As one remains in this state, gradually one becomes totally immersed in the object. The mind, then like a flawless diamond, reflects only the features of the object and nothing else.

In the beginning all mental activities, except sleep, are involved in the comprehension of an object. But, gradually only those needed for correct, flawless comprehension remain.

I.42

तत्र शब्दार्थज्ञानविकल्पैः संकीर्णा सवितर्का समापत्तिः ।

tatra śabdārthajñānavikalpaiḥ saṁkīrṇa savitarkā samāpattiḥ

However, this does not happen spontaneously. It is gradual.

Initially, because of our past experiences and ideas, our understanding of the object is distorted.

Everything that has been heard, read or felt may interfere with our perception.

Some of these influences may have no validity. Others may now be redundant.

I.43

स्मृतिपरिशुद्धौ स्वरूपशून्येवार्थमात्रनिर्भासा निर्वितर्का ।

smṛtipariśuddhau svarūpaśūnyevārthamātranirbhāsā nirvitarkā

When the direction of the mind towards the object is sustained, the ideas and memories of the past gradually recede. The mind becomes crystal clear and is in union with the object. At this moment there is no feeling of oneself. This is pure perception.

I.44

एतयैव सविचारा निर्विचारा च सूक्ष्मविषया व्याख्याता ।

etayaiva savicārā nirvicārā ca sūkṣmaviṣayā vyākhyātā

But, this phenomenon is not limited in scope.

This process is possible with any type of object, at any level of perception, whether superficial and general, or profound and specific.

I.45

सूक्ष्मविषयत्वं चालिङ्गपर्यवसानम् ।

sūkṣmaviṣayatvaṁ cāliṅgaparyavasānam

Except that the mind cannot comprehend the very source of perception within us, its objects can be unlimited.

I.46

ता एव सबीजः समाधिः ।

tā eva sabījaḥ samādhiḥ

Can the mind arrive at a state of Yoga unilaterally?

All these processes of directing the mind involve an object of enquiry.

They also involve preparation, gradual progression and sustained interest. For, without this interest, there will be distraction. Without preparation, there can be no foundation. And without gradual progression, the human system may react and rebel.

I.47

निर्विचारवैशारद्येऽध्यात्मप्रसादः ।

nirvicāravaiśāradye'dhyātmaprasādaḥ

What are the consequences of achieving this ability to direct the mind?

Then the individual begins to truly know himself.

As the correct comprehension of the object begins to enrich us, we also begin to understand our very selves.

I.48

ऋतंभरा तत्र प्रज्ञा ।

ṛtaṁbharā tatra prajñā

Then, what one sees and shares with others is free from error.

I.49

श्रुतानुमानप्रज्ञाभ्यामन्यविषया विशेषार्थत्वात् ।

śrutānumānaprajñābhyāmanyaviṣayā viśeṣārthatvāt

His knowledge is no longer based on memory or inference. It is spontaneous, direct and at a level and intensity that is beyond the ordinary.

In such circumstances, the mind reflects the object of our enquiry simply, like a clear and perfect mirror.

I.50

तज्जः संस्कारोऽन्यसंस्कारप्रतिबन्धी ।

tajjaḥ saṁskāro'nyasaṁskārapratibandhī

As this newly acquired quality of the mind strengthens gradually, it dominates other mental tendencies which are based on misapprehensions.

I.51

तस्यापि निरोधे सर्वनिरोधान्निर्बीजः समाधिः ।

tasyāpi nirodhe sarvanirodhānnirbījaḥ samādhiḥ

Finally, if ever,

The mind reaches a state when it has no impressions of any sort. It is open, clear and simply transparent.

Such comprehension is not sought. It comes inevitably and nothing can stop it.

This is the highest state of Yoga, but it cannot be described in words. Only those who have reached this state can comprehend its nature.

Chapter 2

साधनपादः

Sādhanapādaḥ

The second chapter is called *Sādhanapādaḥ*. It describes the qualities necessary to change the mind effectively and gradually from a state of distraction to one of attention, why these qualities are important and what their practice entails.

II.1

तपःस्वाध्यायेश्वरप्रणिधानानि क्रियायोगः ।

tapaḥsvādhyāyeśvarapraṇidhānāni kriyāyogaḥ

The practice of Yoga must reduce both physical and mental impurities. It must develop our capacity for self examination and help us to understand that in the final analysis, we are not the masters of everything we do.

If the practice of Yoga does not help us remove the symptoms and causes of our physical and mental problems, it cannot lead us on to discovering our inner selves and therefore does not facilitate our understanding of the nature and quality of actions. In such circumstances, the practices will be of doubtful validity. The more we refine ourselves through Yoga the more we realize that all our actions need to be re-examined systematically and that we must not take the fruits of our actions for granted.

II.2

समाधिभावनार्थः क्लेशतनूकरणार्थश्च ।

samādhibhāvanārthaḥ kleśatanūkaraṇārthaśca

Then, such practices will be certain to remove the obstacles to clear perception.

We are all inherently capable of clear perception. But, something or the other frequently seems to come in the way. What are these obstacles?

II.3

अविद्यास्मितारागद्वेषाभिनिवेशाः क्लेशाः ।

avidyāsmitārāgadveṣābhiniveśāḥ kleśāḥ

The obstacles are misapprehension, false identity, excessive attachments, unreasonable dislikes and insecurity.

II.4

अविद्या क्षेत्रमुत्तरेषां प्रसुप्ततनुविच्छिन्नोदाराणाम् ।

avidyā kṣetramuttareṣāṁ prasuptatanuvicchinnodārāṇām

The following ***sūtra*** explains the interrelationships between the above obstacles.

Misapprehension is the source of all the other obstacles. They need not appear simultaneously and their impacts vary. Sometimes they are obscure and barely visible. At other times they are exposed and dominant.

It is only when they are completely exposed, that the effects of these obstacles are evident to other people, although not necessarily to the individual concerned.

II.5

अनित्याशुचिदुःखानात्मसु नित्यशुचिसुखात्मख्यातिरविद्या ।

anityāśuciduḥkhānātmasu nityaśucisukhātmakhyātiravidyā

The following ***sūtra-s*** describe the five obstacles listed above -

Misapprehension leads to errors in comprehension of the character, origin and effects of the objects perceived.

What at one time may appear to be beneficial may turn out to be a problem at a later stage. What we seek as a source of pleasure may turn out to have the opposite effect. Fool's gold is assumed to be gold. Things that must change, like the beauty of youth, may be considered everlasting. What might be considered as the most important learning, may, in time, prove useless.

II.6

दृग्दर्शनशक्त्योरेकात्मतेवास्मिता ।

dṛgdarśanaśaktyorekātmatevāsmitā

False identity results when we regard mental activity as the very source of perception.

Mental attitudes and activities change. They modify themselves according to influences such as moods, habits and surroundings. Yet, somehow we often assume that they are constant, unchanging sources of perception. See II – 20.

II.7

सुखानुशयी रागः ।

sukhānuśayī rāgaḥ

Excessive attachment is based on the assumption that it will contribute to everlasting happiness.

When an object satisfies a desire, it provides a moment of happiness. Hence, the possession of objects can become very important, even indispensable whatever the cost. The result may be future unhappiness and the loss of some essentials of life.

II.8

दुःखानुशयी द्वेषः ।

duḥkhānuśayī dveṣaḥ

Unreasonable dislikes are usually the result of painful experiences in the past, connected with particular objects and situations.

These dislikes continue to persist even after the circumstances that caused the unpleasant experiences have changed or disappeared.

II.9

स्वरसवाही विदुषोऽपि समारूढोऽभिनिवेशः ।

svarasavāhī viduṣo'pi samārūḍho'bhiniveśaḥ

Insecurity is the inborn feeling of anxiety about what is to come. It affects both the ignorant and the wise.

This syndrome may have a reasonable base in past experiences. It may be completely irrational. It does not disappear even when we know that death is imminent. It is, perhaps, the most difficult obstacle to overcome.

II.10

ते प्रतिप्रसवहेयाः सूक्ष्माः ।

te pratiprasavaheyāḥ sūkṣmāḥ

Having described the obstacles that prevent clear perception, *Patañjali* indicates what the attitude of one who is keen on overcoming them should be.

When the obstacles do not seem to be present, it is important to be vigilant.

A temporary state of clarity should not be confused with a permanent state. To assume then, that everything will be free from now on, can be fraught with danger. It is now even more important to be careful. The fall from clarity to confusion is more disturbing than a state with no clarity at all.

II.11

ध्यानहेयास्तद्वृत्तयः ।

dhyānaheyāstadvṛttayaḥ

However, when there is evidence that obstacles are reappearing, immediately

Advance towards a state of reflection to reduce their impact and prevent them from taking over.

Any means that will help us free ourselves from the consequences of these obstacles is acceptable. This could be a prayer, a discussion with a teacher or a diversion. *Patañjali* has suggested a number of means in the first chapter (I – 23, I – 30, I – 39) and more follow.

II.12

क्लेशमूलः कर्माशयो दृष्टादृष्टजन्मवेदनीयः ।

kleśamūlaḥ karmāśayo dṛṣṭādṛṣṭajanmavedanīyaḥ

Why should we be so concerned about these obstacles?

Our actions and their consequences are influenced by these obstacles. The consequences may or may not be evident at the time of the action.

These obstacles are based in the mind and in the body as well. All our actions emanate from them. Those actions which are initiated when the obstacles are dominant will certainly produce undesirable results. For, the obstacles are based on misapprehension. When we mistake what we see, the conclusions drawn from what we see must be incorrect. The next *sūtra* goes into this in greater detail.

II.13

सति मूले तद्विपाको जात्यायुर्भोगाः ।

sati mūle tadvipāko jātyāyurbhogāḥ

As long as the obstacles prevail, they will affect action in every respect-in its execution, duration and consequences.

Obstacles may lead to the faulty execution of actions. They may influence our mental attitudes during the process of taking action and perhaps reduce or extend their timespan. And finally, the fruits of actions may be such that they contribute to existing problems or create new ones.

II.14

ते ह्लादपरितापफलाः पुण्यापुण्यहेतुत्वात् ।

te hlādaparitāpaphalāḥ puṇyāpuṇyahetutvāt

Does it follow that all our actions can lead to problems of some sort?

The consequences of an action will be painful or beneficial depending on whether the obstacles were present in the conception or implementation of the action.

If the obstacles are dormant during the initiation and execution of an action, there is enough clarity to perceive the correct attitude and means of acting and thus avoid mistakes. However, if they are active, there cannot be enough clarity and the consequences can be undesirable or painful.

II.15

परिणामतापसंस्कारदुःखैर्गुणवृत्तिविरोधाच्च
दुःखमेव सर्वं विवेकिनः ।

pariṇāmatāpasaṁskāraduḥkhairguṇavṛttivirodhācca duḥkhameva sarvaṁ vivekinaḥ

What is the cause of unpleasant or painful effects?

Painful effects from any object or situation can be a result of one or more of the following - changes in the perceived object, the desire to repeat pleasurable experiences and the strong effect of conditioning from the past. In addition, changes within the individual can be contributory factors.

There is a constant change of some sort in ourselves and in the objects of our senses. These changes may be unrecognized. Thus, we may have an urge to seek for more of the same, when there is no possibility of achieving this. The effects of past conditioning can create strong reactions if what we are used to is not forthcoming. We must add to this the complexity of the patterns of ourselves in relation to the world around us. Thus, there is potential in any object or situation to contribute to painful or unpleasant effects. What can we do?

II.16

हेयं दुःखमनागतम् ।

heyaṁ duḥkhamanāgatam

Painful effects which are likely to occur should be anticipated and avoided

Whatever helps us to anticipate or reduce painful effects must be done. *Patañjali* goes on to present the causes of such painful effects and what we can do to develop within ourselves the capacity to anticipate, prevent, reduce or accept them. In brief, the practice of Yoga, has as its purpose the reduction of painful effects on ourselves by increasing our clarity. This means that we must learn to contain and control the obstacles listed in *sūtra* II – 3.

II.17

द्रष्टृदृश्ययोः संयोगो हेयहेतुः ।

draṣṭṛdṛśyayoḥ saṁyogo heyahetuḥ

The primary cause of the actions that produce painful effects is now presented.

The cause of actions that produce painful effects is the inability to distinguish what is perceived from what perceives.

In each of us, there exists an entity that perceives. This is quite distinct from what is perceived, such as the mind, the body, the senses and the objects. But, often we do not make this distinction. What is perceived is subject to changes, but we do not recognize these changes. This lack of clear understanding can produce painful effects, even without us recognizing them.

II.18

प्रकाशक्रियास्थितिशीलं भूतेन्द्रियात्मकं भोगापवर्गार्थं दृश्यम् ।

prakāśakriyāsthitiśīlaṁ bhūtendriyātmakaṁ bhogāpavargārthaṁ dṛśyam

What distinguishes the objects of perception from that which perceives? The following *sūtra-s* explain this

All that is perceived includes not only the external objects but also the mind and the senses. They share three qualities - heaviness, activity and clarity. They have two types of effects - to expose the perceiver to their influences or to provide the means to find the distinction between them and itself.

All that is perceived has the capacity to display the three qualities mentioned above, but they vary in intensity and degree. The nature of their effects on us is explored further in the next few *sūtra-s.*

II.19

विशेषाविशेषलिङ्गमात्रालिङ्गानि गुणपर्वाणि ।

viśeṣāviśeṣaliṅgamātrāliṅgāni guṇaparvāṇi

All that is perceived is related by the common sharing of the three qualities.

In addition, they affect each other. For instance, what we eat influences our state of mind. Our state of mind affects our attitude to our bodies and to our enviroment.

II.20

द्रष्टा दृशिमात्रः शुद्धोऽपि प्रत्ययानुपश्यः ।

draṣṭā dṛśimātraḥ śuddho'pi pratyayānupaśyaḥ

What is it that perceives?

That which perceives is not subject to any variations. But, it always perceives through the mind

Consequently, the quality of perception is affected by the state of the mind which is the instrument of perception. The color of an object is affected by the color of glass through which it is seen. In the same way, whether there is perception or not, whether it is correct or incorrect, depends on the state of mind.

II.21

तदर्थ एव दृश्यस्यात्मा ।

tadartha eva dṛśyasyātmā

All that can be perceived has but one purpose - to be perceived.

In this way they serve the perceiver but have no individuality of their own. Their purpose comes from their perception by a perceiver. This can be compared to food placed on the table, which is there for the guest and not for its own sake.

II.22

कृतार्थं प्रति नष्टमप्यनष्टं तदन्यसाधारणत्वात् ।

kṛtārthaṁ prati naṣṭamapyanaṣṭaṁ
tadanyasādhāraṇatvāt

Does this mean that without a perceiver, the objects of perception do not exist?

The existence of all objects of perception and their appearance is independent of the needs of the individual perceiver. They exist without individual reference, to cater to the different needs of different individuals.

The needs of an individual may only be defined at a particular time. Some needs may be periodic or spasmodic. And the needs of one individual cannot be considered more important, in terms of quality and justification, than those of another.

A car may be required not by the owner, but by the owner's spouse. Food may not be needed now, but in a few hours it may be essential. Does the food on the table vanish if the guest does not arrive?

II.23

स्वस्वामिशक्त्योः स्वरूपोपलब्धिहेतुः संयोगः ।

svasvāmiśaktyoḥ svarūpopalabdhihetuḥ saṁyogaḥ

In addition,

All that is perceived, whatever it is and whatever its effect on a particular individual, has but one ultimate purpose. That is to clarify the distinction between the external that is seen and the internal that sees.

However powerful or disturbing something may appear to be, it is our reaction to it that determines its effects. Therefore, we can, by identifying and differenciating between what perceives and what is perceived, what sees and what is seen, put the object in its correct perspective and determine its effect and influence on us.

II.24

तस्य हेतुरविद्या ।

tasya heturavidyā

Why, on occasion, is clarity absent?

The absence of clarity in distinguishing between what perceives and what is perceived is due to the accumulation of misapprehension.

II.25

तदभावात्संयोगाभावो हानं तद्दृशेः कैवल्यम् ।

tadabhāvātsaṁyogābhāvo hānaṁ taddṛśeḥ kaivalyam

As misapprehension is reduced there is a corresponding increase in clarity. This is the path to freedom.

Yes, this is the ultimate goal of Yoga practice. Freedom is the absence of the consequences of obstacles and the avoidance of actions which have distracting or disturbing effects.

II.26

विवेकख्यातिरविप्लवा हानोपायः ।

vivekakhyātiraviplavā hānopāyaḥ

How do we achieve this freedom? Is it really possible?

Essentially the means must be directed towards developing clarity so that the distinction between the changing qualities of what is perceived and the unchanging quality of what perceives becomes evident.

This requires constant effort. This effort must reduce the persistent intrusion of the obstacles listed in *sūtra* II – 3 and eventually eliminate their effects completely . Once a beginning is made, the foundation of Yoga is laid.

II.27

तस्य सप्तधा प्रान्तभूमिः प्रज्ञा ।

tasya saptadhā prāntabhūmiḥ prajñā

The attainment of clarity is a gradual process.

The first step is to recognize that certain tendencies of the mind are responsible for producing painful effects. If these tendencies are not curtailed, we may reach a point of no return.

II.28

योगाङ्गानुष्ठानादशुद्धिक्षये ज्ञानदीप्तिराविवेकख्यातेः ।

yogāṅgānuṣṭhānādaśuddhikṣaye jñānadīptirāvivekakhyāteḥ

Can something be done to recognize and correct these tendencies? *Patañjali* proposes some definitive means for reducing the accumulation of obstacles such as misapprehension. For, only the reduction of these obstacles can reverse the tendencies responsible for producing undesirable effects.

Practice and enquiry into different components of Yoga gradually reduce obstacles such as misapprehension (II – 3). Then, the lamp of perception brightens and the distinction between what perceives and what is perceived becomes increasingly evident. Now everything can be understood without error.

If the mind is cleared of the obstacles that cloud true perception, there can be no errors or flaws in perception. Actions are thus free from regrettable consequences.

Patañjali presents the components of Yoga as follows

II.29

यमनियमासनप्राणायामप्रत्याहारधारणाध्यानसमाधयोऽष्टावङ्गानि ।

yamaniyamāsanaprāṇāyāmapratyāhāradhāraṇā dhyānasamādhayo'ṣṭāvaṅgāni

There are eight components of Yoga. These are -

1. *Yama – our attitudes towards our environment.*
2. *Niyama – our attitudes towards ourselves.*
3. *Āsana – the practice of body exercises.*
4. *Prāṇāyāma – the practice of breathing exercises*
5. *Pratyāhāra – restraint of our senses.*
6. *Dhāraṇā – the ability to direct the mind.*
7. *Dhyāna – the ability to develop interactions with what we seek to understand.*
8. *Samādhi – complete integration with the object to be understood.*

The order of presentation moves from external relationships to a very intense and refined state of introspection. However, this order is not necessarily the sequence to be followed in practice. There are no set rules or definitive routes. The route that is most suited for the individual to reach the state described in *sūtra* I. 2 should be followed. All these components develop simultaneously as the individual progresses.

II.30

अहिंसासत्यास्तेयब्रह्मचर्यापरिग्रहा यमाः ।

ahiṁsāsatyāsteyabrahmacaryāparigrahā yamāḥ

The eight components of Yoga are discussed in the following *sūtra-s*.

Yama comprises:

1. *Consideration towards all living beings, especially those who are innocent, in difficulty, or worse off than we are.*
2. *Right communication through speech, writing, gesture and actions.*
3. *Noncovetousness or the ability to resist a desire for that which does not belong to us.*
4. *Moderation in all our actions.*
5. *Absence of greed or the ability to accept only what is appropriate.*

How we exhibit these qualities and how we strive for them depends inevitably on our social and cultural background and our individual characteristics and potentials. But, their representation in an individual is a reflection of the extent to which the obstacles in the mind are at work. How we behave towards others and our environment reveals our state of mind and our personalities. The nature of the knock at the door indicates the character of the visitor!

II.31

जातिदेशकालसमयानवच्छिन्नाः सार्वभौमा महाव्रतम् ।

jātideśakālasamayānavacchinnāḥ sārvabhaumā mahāvratam

When the adoption of these attitudes to our environment is beyond compromise, regardless of our social, cultural, intellectual or individual station, it approaches irreversibility.

We cannot begin with such attitudes. If we adopt them abruptly we cannot sustain them. We can always find excuses for not maintaining them. But, if we seek to identify the reasons why we hold contrary views and isolate the obstacles that permit such views, our attitudes will gradually change. The obstacles will give way and our behaviour towards others and our environment will change for the better.

II.32

शौचसंतोषतपःस्वाध्यायेश्वरप्रणिधानानि नियमाः ।

śaucasaṁtoṣatapaḥsvādhyāyeśvarapraṇidhānāni niyamāḥ

Niyama comprises:

1. *Cleanliness, or the keeping of our bodies and our surroundings neat and clean.*
2. *Contentment or the ability to be happy with what we have and do not crave what we do not have.*

3. *The removal of impurities in our physical and mental systems through the maintenance of correct habits such as sleep, exercise, nutrition, work and relaxation.*
4. *Study and the necessity to review and evaluate our progress.*
5. *Actions done more in the spirit of service than for personal gain.*

As with our attitudes to others and our environment, these priorities establish themselves and the correct attitudes develop concurrently with our rectification of errors and actions which cause problems.

II.33

वितर्कबाधने प्रतिपक्षभावनम् ।

vitarkabādhane pratipakṣabhāvanam

How can we examine and re-examine our attitudes to others?

When these attitudes are questioned, self reflection on the possible consequences of alternative attitudes may help.

Therefore, we must find a means to examine intellectually, the consequences of different possible attitudes at a given time or under given circumstances. To look before we leap!

II.34

वितर्का हिंसादयः कृतकारितानुमोदिता लोभक्रोधमोहपूर्वका मृदुमध्याधिमात्रा दुःखाज्ञानानन्तफला इति प्रतिपक्षभावनम् ।

vitarkā hiṁsādayaḥ kṛtakāritānumoditā lobhakrodhamohapūrvakā mṛdumadhyādhimātrā duḥkhājñānānantaphalā iti pratipakṣabhāvanam

Patañjali explains this further.

For example, a sudden desire to act harshly, or to encourage or approve of harsh actions, can be contained by reflecting on the harmful consequences. Often, such actions are the results of lower instincts such as anger, possessiveness and unsound judgement. Whether these actions are minor or major, reflection in a suitable atmosphere can contain the desire to act in this way.

Often, some of our attitudes towards people, situations and ideas are not very clear. Then, a hasty step may land us in situations we do not want to be in. In such circumstances any opportunity to have second thoughts is worth considering. Prevention is always better than cure.

II.35

अहिंसाप्रतिष्ठायां तत्सन्निधौ वैरत्यागः ।

ahiṁsāpratiṣṭhāyāṁ tatsannidhau vairatyāgaḥ

We must remember that there are individual variations. Some of us may be quite comfortable examining our motives and attitudes. Others may find it very difficult to reflect upon themselves. *Patañjali* now indicates signs of progress in each of the ten attitudes listed in *sūtra-s* II – 30 and II – 32.

The more considerate one is, the more one stimulates friendly feelings among all in one's presence.

Even those who are unfriendly at other times and among other people may show a different aspect and be friendly in our presence.

II.36

सत्यप्रतिष्ठायां क्रियाफलाश्रयत्वम् ।

satyapratiṣṭhāyāṁ kriyāphalāśrayatvam

One who shows a high degree of right communication, will not fail in his actions.

The ability to be honest in communicating with sensitivity, without hurting others, without telling lies and with the necessary reflection, requires a very refined state of being. Such persons cannot make mistakes in their actions.

II.37

अस्तेयप्रतिष्ठायां सर्वरत्नोपस्थानम् ।

asteyapratiṣṭhāyāṁ sarvaratnopasthānam

One who is trustworthy, because he does not covet what belongs to others, naturally has every one's confidence and everything is shared with him, however precious it might be.

II.38

ब्रह्मचर्यप्रतिष्ठायां वीर्यलाभः ।

brahmacaryapratiṣṭhāyāṁ vīryalābhaḥ

At its best, moderation produces the highest individual vitality.

Nothing is wanted by us if we seek to develop moderation in all things. Too much of anything results in problems. Too little may be inadequate.

II.39

अपरिग्रहस्थैर्ये जन्मकथंतासंबोधः ।

aparigrahasthairye janmakathaṁtāsaṁbodhaḥ

One who is not greedy is secure. He has time to think deeply. His understanding of himself is complete.

The more we have, the more we need to take care of it. The time and energy spent on acquiring more things, protecting them and worrying about them cannot be spent on the basic questions of life. What is the limit to what we should possess? For what purpose, for whom and for how long? Death comes before we have had time to even begin considering these questions.

II.40

शौचात्स्वाङ्गजुगुप्सा परैरसंसर्गः ।

śaucātsvāṅgajugupsā parairasaṁsargaḥ

When cleanliness is developed, it reveals what needs to be constantly maintained and what is eternally clean. What decays is the external. What does not is deep within us.

Our excessive concern about and attachment to outward things, which are both transient and superficial, is reduced.

II.41

सत्त्वशुद्धिसौमनस्यैकाग्र्येन्द्रियजयात्मदर्शनयोग्यत्वानि च ।

***sattvaśuddhisaumanasyaikāgryendriya-
jayātmadarśanayogyatvāni ca***

In addition, we are able to reflect on the profound nature of our individual selves, including the source of perception, without being distracted by the senses, and with freedom from misapprehensions accumulated from the past.

To regard outward objects as the most valuable and to guard them at all costs is not the most important part of life. There is much more to look into. Dirty clothes may make a person look ugly. But they can be changed. However, if there is dirt deep inside, it cannot be removed so easily.

II.42

संतोषादनुत्तमः सुखलाभः ।

saṁtoṣādanuttamaḥ sukhalābhaḥ

The result of contentment is total happiness.

The happiness we get from acquiring possessions is only temporary. We need to constantly find and acquire new possessions to sustain this sort of happiness. There is no end to it. But, true contentment, leading to total happiness and bliss, is in a class of its own.

II.43

कायेन्द्रियसिद्धिरशुद्धिक्षयात्तपसः ।

kāyendriyasiddhiraśuddhikṣayāttapasaḥ

The removal of impurities allows the body to function more efficiently.

Both physical and mental ailments and disabilities are contained.

II.44

स्वाध्यायादिष्टदेवतासंप्रयोगः ।

svādhyāyādiṣṭadevatāsaṁprayogaḥ

Study, when it is developed to the highest degree, brings one close to the higher Source that promotes understanding of the most complex.

The more effective our study, the more we understand our weaknesses and strengths. We learn to nullify our weaknesses and use our strengths to the maximum. Then, there is no limit to our understanding.

II.45

समाधिसिद्धिरीश्वरप्रणिधानात् ।

samādhisiddhirīśvarapraṇidhānāt

Actions done in the spirit of service promote the ability to completely understand any object of choice.

Then, to direct the mind towards any object of any complexity is not a problem.

II.46

स्थिरसुखमासनम् ।

sthirasukhamāsanam

Āsana and *prāṇāyāma*, the next two aspects of Yoga (see *sūtra* II – 29) are now presented as they help us to understand and use correctly and appropriately our bodies and breath. They are easier to begin with, unlike changing our attitudes. With them it is possible for most of us to begin reducing the obstacles to Yoga. The instructions given here are brief because the practices must be learnt directly from a competent teacher.

Āsana must have the dual qualities of alertness and relaxation.

Āsana practice involves body exercises. When they are properly practiced there must be alertness without tension and relaxation without dullness or heaviness.

II.47

प्रयत्नशैथिल्यानन्तसमापत्तिभ्याम् ।

prayatnaśaithilyānantasamāpattibhyām

These qualities can be achieved by recognizing and observing the reactions of the body and the breath to the various postures that comprise āsana practice. Once known, these reactions can be controlled step by step.

II.48

तततो द्वन्द्वानभिघातः ।

tato dvandvānabhighātaḥ

When these principles are correctly followed, ***āsana*** *practice will help a person endure and even minimize external influences such as age, climate, diet and work on the body.*

This is the beginning of the reduction of the effect of obstacles such as misapprehension; for the body expresses what is in the mind. Practices such as *āsana* begin to rectify the harmful consequences of the obstacles at the level of the body. The well-being so developed opens us up to the possibilities of further understanding of ourselves. If we have a backache, the need for relief from this pain dominates our thoughts. If, through our efforts at *āsana* practice, we reduce this backache, we can then begin to explore the cause of the pain.

II.49

तस्मिन्सतिश्वासप्रश्वासयोर्गतिविच्छेदः प्राणायामः ।

tasminsatiśvāsapraśvāsayorgativicchedaḥ prāṇāyāmaḥ

Through *āsana* practice, we can also understand how the breath behaves. Breathing patterns vary from individual to individual. They can vary as a result of our state of mind or bodily changes as a result of both internal and external forces. This knowledge of breath, gained through *āsana* practice, is the foundation for beginning *prāṇāyāma* practice.

Prāṇāyāma is the conscious, deliberate regulation of the breath, replacing unconscious patterns of breathing. It is possible only after a resonable mastery of āsana practice.

This practice is usually done in a comfortable but erect, seated position.

II.50

बाह्याभ्यन्तरस्तम्भवृत्तिर्देशकालसंख्याभिः परिदृष्टो दीर्घसूक्ष्मः ।

bāhyābhyantarastambhavṛttirdeśakālasaṁkhyābhiḥ paridṛṣṭo dīrghasūkṣmaḥ

What are the components of *prāṇāyāma*?

It involves the regulation of exhalation, inhalation and suspension of the breath. The regulation of these three processes is achieved by modulating their lengths, and maintaining this modulation for a period of time, as well as focusing the mind on the process. These components of breathing must be both long and uniform.

Many combinations are possible in the practice of *prāṇāyāma*. Many techniques are available, but details about these are beyond the scope of this text.

II.51

बाह्याभ्यन्तरविषयाक्षेपी चतुर्थः ।

bāhyābhyantaraviṣayākṣepī caturthaḥ

An entirely different state of breathing appears in the state of Yoga.

Then the breath transcends the level of the consciousness.

It is not possible to be more specific.

II.52

ततः क्षीयते प्रकाशावरणम् ।

tataḥ kṣīyate prakāśāvaraṇam

The results of *prāṇāyāma* practice are indicated.

The regular practice of prāṇāyāma reduces the obstacles that inhibit clear perception.

II.53

धारणासु च योग्यता मनसः ।

dhāraṇāsu ca yogyatā manasaḥ

And the mind is now prepared for the process of direction towards a chosen goal.

II.54

स्वविषयासंप्रयोगे चित्तस्य स्वरूपानुकार इवेन्द्रियाणां प्रत्याहारः ।

svaviṣayāsaṁprayoge cittasya svarūpānukāra ivendriyāṇāṁ pratyāhāraḥ

The restraint of the senses, *pratyāhāra,* which is the fifth aspect of Yoga (see II – 29) is now defined.

Restraint of the senses occurs when the mind is able to remain in its chosen direction and the senses disregard the different objects around them and faithfully follow the direction of the mind.

II.55

ततः परमा वश्यतेन्द्रियाणाम् ।

tataḥ paramā vaśyatendriyāṇām

Then the senses are mastered.

The senses cooperate in the chosen enquiry instead of being a cause of distraction. Restraint of the senses cannot be a strict discipline. It develops, as the obstacles to perception within us are cleared up.

Chapter 3

विभूतिपादः
Vibhūtipādaḥ

In this chapter, *Vibhūtipādaḥ*, *Patañjali* describes the capacity of the mind, which, through the various practices described in the earlier two chapters can achieve a state free from distractions. Such a mind can probe deeply into objects and concepts. Indeed, there are innumerable possibilities for it. Then, there arises in the individual a knowledge of the objects of a dimension previously unknown. However, even such knowledge can itself be a source of distraction and prevent a person from reaching the highest state of being. This highest state is freedom from disturbance of any sort and at any time. The next three *sūtra-s* describe the sixth, seventh and eighth components of Yoga first mentioned in *sūtra* (II-29). The first five components are described in chapter II.

III.1

देशबन्धश्चित्तस्य धारणा ।

deśabandhaścittasya dhāraṇā

The mind has reached the ability to be directed (dhāranā) when direction towards a chosen object is possible in spite of many other potential objects within the reach of the individual.

The object is chosen by the individual regardless of the attraction of alternatives. The chosen object may be sensual or conceptual, simple or complex, tangible or beyond touch, in favorable conditions or against all odds. The ability to maintain direction in this way is not possible if our minds are immersed in distractions or strongly affected by obstacles such as misapprehension (see *sūtra* II – 3).

III.2

तत्र प्रत्ययैकतानता ध्यानम् ।

tatra pratyayaikatānatā dhyānam

Once the direction is fixed, a link develops between the mind's activities and the chosen object.

Then the mental activities form an uninterrupted flow only in relation to this object.

Initially our understanding is influenced by misapprehension, imagination and memories. But, as the process of comprehension intensifies, it freshens and deepens our understanding of the object.

III.3

तदेवार्थमात्रनिर्भासं स्वरूपशून्यमिव समाधिः ।

tadevārthamātranirbhāsaṁ svarūpaśūnyamiva samādhiḥ

Soon, the individual is so involved in the object, that nothing except its comprehension is evident. It is as if the individual has lost his own identity. This is complete integration with the object of understanding (samādhi).

When we reach this state, all that is evident is the object itself. We are not even aware that we are distinct beings separate from the object. Our mental activities are integrated with the object and nothing else.

III.4

त्रयमेकत्र संयमः ।

trayamekatra saṁyamaḥ

The three processes described in *sūtra-s* III – 1, III – 2 and III – 3 can be employed with different objects at different times, or they can all be directed for an indefinite period of time on the same object.

When these processes are continuously and exclusively applied to the same object it is called ***saṁyama.***

III.5

तज्जयात्प्रज्ञालोकः ।

tajjayātprajñālokaḥ

What results from this continuous and exclusive practice of *saṁyama*?

Saṁyama *on a chosen object leads to a comprehensive knowledge of the object in all its aspects*

III.6

तस्य भूमिषु विनियोगः ।

tasya bhūmiṣu viniyogaḥ

Can any object be selected for directing the mind into the process of *saṁyama*? What is the basis for our choice?

Saṁyama *must be developed gradually.*

The object of *saṁyama* must be chosen with due appreciation of our potential for such enquiry. We should begin with less complicated objects and with those which can be enquired into in several different ways. Then, there is a greater chance of successful development. It is implied that a teacher who knows us well is a great help in choosing our objects.

III.7

त्रयमन्तरङ्गं पूर्वेभ्यः ।

trayamantaraṅgaṁ pūrvebhyaḥ

To specify what is easy for one individual is not possible in *saṁyama* or any other practice. *Patañjali* presents the idea of relativity. Everything is relative.

*Compared to the first five components of Yoga (**sūtra** II – 29) The next three (**sūtra-s** III – 1,2,3) are more intricate.*

The first five components of yoga are our attitude towards our environment, our attitude towards ourselves, the practice of body exercises (*āsana*), the practice of breathing exercises (*prāṇāyāma*), and restraint of the senses (*pratyāhara*). They are easier to understand and attempt than the next three aspects. These are the ability to direct our minds (*dhārana*), the ability to develop faultlessly our interactions with what we seek to understand (*dhyāna*), and complete integration with the object of our understanding (*samādhi*).

III.8

तदपि बहिरङ्गं निर्बीजस्य ।

tadapi bahiraṅgaṁ nirbījasya

If we develop our capacities, we can, through sustained

discipline, refine and adapt our minds sufficiently to facilitate the process of directing them without difficulty.

The state where the mind has no impressions of any sort and nothing is beyond its reach (nirbīja samādhi) is more intricate than the state of directing the mind towards an object (samādhi).

Sūtra I – 51 defines this, the highest state of Yoga. The mind in this state is simply transparent, devoid of any resistance to enquiry and free from past impressions of any sort.

The message of *sūtra-s* III – 7 and III – 8 is that *saṁyama* is only possible at our own individual levels. There can be no universal gradation in choosing the direction of enquiry. It cannot be at the same level for all of us at all times. This is the relative aspect of *saṁyama,* for it is based on each individual's capacity and needs. Some of us may, in other ways, have developed capacities which enable us to begin *saṁyama* at a higher level than others. An expert on human anatomy does not need to study much to understand the vertebral column of a horse. But, an expert in finance might have to begin with a study of basic anatomy.

III.9

व्युत्थाननिरोधसंस्कारयोरभिभवप्रादुर्भावौ
निरोधक्षणचित्तान्वयो निरोधपरिणामः ।

vyutthānanirodhasaṁskārayorabhibhavaprādurbhāvau nirodhakṣaṇacittānvayo nirodhapariṇāmaḥ

How can our minds, which are used to one way of operating, be changed? *Patañjali* tackles this question by showing that everything we perceive is subject to modification. More than this, everything can be modified in a chosen way.

The mind is capable of having two states based on two distinct tendencies. These are distraction and attention. However, at any one moment, only one state prevails, and this state influences the individuals's behaviour, attitudes and expressions.

When the state of attention prevails, our poise is serene, our breathing quiet and our concentration on our object is such that we are completely absorbed in it and oblivious of our surroundings. But, when we are in the state of distraction, our poise is far from serene, our breathing is irregular and our attitude gives little indication of any capacity to be attentive.

III.10

तस्य प्रशान्तवाहिता संस्कारात् ।

tasya praśāntavāhitā saṁskārāt

Can we develop the state of attention?

With constant and uninterrupted practice, the mind can remain in a state of attention for a long time.

But, if we do not attempt to sustain this state, then the state of distraction takes over.

III.11

सर्वार्थतैकाग्रतयोः क्षयोदयौ चित्तस्य समाधिपरिणामः ।

sarvārthataikāgratayoḥ kṣayodayau cittasya samādhipariṇāmaḥ

Even the quality of distraction can vary and be modified. The mind can be chaotic, or it can be so heavy that it cannot be disturbed or it can be very susceptible to disturbance. These variations depend upon our past tendencies and how we have responded to them. There is another intermediate state of being.

The mind alternates between the possibility of intense concentration and a state where alternative objects can attract attention.

The difference between the previous situation and this one is that while in the former, the mind alternated between two quite different and opposite states, in this case the difference between the two alternating states is lesser. There is, therefore, a greater chance to return to the fixed direction of enquiry without too much loss of time and without the lasting effects of the distracted state of mind.

III.12

ततः पुनः शान्तोदितौ तुल्यप्रत्ययौ चित्तस्यैकाग्रतापरिणामः ।

tataḥ punaḥ śāntoditau tulyapratyayau cittasyaikāgratāpariṇāmaḥ

With further refinement of our minds

The mind reaches a stage in which the link with the object is consistent and continuous. The distractions cease to appear.

Then, our relationship with the object is no longer disrupted by the other tendencies of the mind. Complete comprehension of the object is definite.

III.13

एतेन भूतेन्द्रियेषु धर्मलक्षणावस्थापरिणामा व्याख्याताः ।

etena bhūtendriyeṣu dharmalakṣaṇāvasthāpariṇāmā vyākhyātāḥ

Thus, it is clear that our minds can have different characteristics. These characteristics are also subject to change. The mind, the senses and the objects of the senses share three basic characteristics - heaviness, activity and clarity. In some ways, most of the changes in our mind are possible because these three qualities are in a state of constant flux. How they change, when they change and what combinations produce the different characteristics of the mind is a complex subject. However,

As it has been established that the mind has different states (corresponding to which there arise different attitudes, possibilities and behavioural patterns in the individual) it can also be said that such changes can occur in all the subjects of perception and in the senses. These changes can be at different levels and are influenced by external forces such as time or our intelligence.

Time can change a fresh flower into a few dry petals. A gold smith can change a nugget of gold into a delicate pendant. A metallurgist can convert it yet again to a compound capable of storing very corrosive fluids. Those characteristics that are apparent at one moment cannot be the whole story of the object. But, if all the potential of, for instance, gold is known, then many products can be produced even though they may have quite different properties. The same is true of the body and the senses. The manual skills of an artist are quite different from those of a car mechanic. The reasoning of a philosopher is different from that of a businessman.

III.14

शान्तोदिताव्यपदेश्यधर्मानुपाती धर्मी ।

śāntoditāvyapadeśyadharmānupātī dharmī

All these different characteristics must be housed somewhere in some form or other.

A substance contains all its charateristics, and depending on the particular form it takes, those characteristics conforming to that form will be apparent. But whatever the form, whatever the characteristics exhibited, there exists a base that comprises all characteristics. Some have appeared in the past, some are currently apparent and others may reveal themselves in the future.

The significance of ***sūtra-s*** III – 9 to III – 14 is that everything we perceive is fact and not fiction. But these facts are subject to change.

III.15

क्रमान्यत्वं परिणामान्यत्वे हेतुः ।

kramānyatvaṁ pariṇāmānyatve hetuḥ

Can these changes in the characteristics of substances be influenced?

By changing the order or sequence of change, characteristics that are of one pattern can be modified to a different pattern

Change has a sequence, but this sequence can be altered. A river flowing across a valley can be diverted through a tunnel. The intelligence to grasp this possibility is what produces the different patterns of change.

III.16

परिणामत्रयसंयमादतीतानागतज्ञानम् ।

pariṇāmatrayasaṁyamādatītānāgatajñānam

In a way, *saṁyama* is the process of changing our mental potential from incomplete, erroneous comprehension of an object, or no comprehension at all, to total comprehension. When this potential is developed, the individual can choose any object for developing a deep knowledge about it.

These objects can be external, within the limits of sensual perception or concepts like change, time or communication. In the following *sūtra-s*, examples are given of such knowledge resulting from different *saṁyama-s.* Whether we are interested in using our highly developed minds to acquire deep knowledge of a specific nature or whether we are more concerned with true freedom is an individual choice. True freedom is more than expertise, it is a state in which all our actions are such that they do not cause repentance or regret. *Patañjali* cautions us about the misuse of *saṁyama* elsewhere.

The first example of directing the mind through *saṁyama* follows.

Saṁyama on the process of change, how it can be affected by time and other factors, develops knowledge of the past and the future.

In *sūtra-s* III – 9 to III – 14, the changes that occur in objects and the senses as well as in the mind are explained. If we pursue this idea in depth, we will be in a position to anticipate what may happen in a particular situation and what has happened in the past. Astronomy is a classic example of this

III.17

शब्दार्थप्रत्ययानामितरेतराध्यासात्संकरस्तत्प्रविभाग -

संयमात्सर्वभूतरुतज्ञानम् ।

śabdārthapratyayānāmitaretarādhyāsātsaṁkaras-
-tatpravibhāga-
-saṁyamātsarvabhūtarutajñānam

Patañjali takes up the process of communication for *saṁyama*. Different symbols and languages exist for relating to other people. These symbols and languages are affected by use, abuse and misinterpretations. Languages serve to explain something that was experienced, may be experienced or is being experienced. An object is an entity in itself. Our ability to see an object is based on our interests and potentials. Our memories and imaginations can influence our comprehension. Therefore, there is ample scope for us to communicate improperly, no matter how much we try.

Saṁyama on the interactions between language, ideas and objects is to examine the individual features of the objects, the means of describing them and the ideas and their cultural influences in the minds of the describers. Through this, one can find the most accurate and effective way of communication regardless of linguistic, cultural and other barriers.

III.18

संस्कारसाक्षात्करणात्पूर्वजातिज्ञानम् ।

saṁskārasākṣātkaraṇātpūrvajātijñānam

In all areas of human activity there is the potential to develop individual habits and tendencies. Some will be more obvious than others.

Saṁyama on one's tendencies and habits will lead one to his/her origins. Consequently, one gains deep knowledge of one's past.

We learn how our behaviour and personal characteristics developed and what events in the past influenced our attitudes, likes and dislikes. We learn to what degree these are related to our heredity, tradition, social requirements, etc. When these roots are known, we can re – examine our life styles better.

III.19

प्रत्ययस्य परचित्तज्ञानम् ।

pratyayasya paracittajñānam

Every mental activity produces distinct physical effects. For example, our physical features, posture and breathing vary when we are sleeping or when we are angry.

Saṁyama on the changes that arise in an individual's mind and their consequences, develops in one the ability to acutely observe the state of mind of others.

Then, we can see how others' states of mind are developing. Physical expressions, rates of breathing and other indicators will reveal turbulence, confusion, doubt, fear, etc.

III.20

न च तत्सालम्बनं तस्याविषयीभूतत्वात् ।

na ca tatsālambanaṁ tasyāviṣayībhūtatvāt

But, can we see from this, what the origin is of the state of mind?

No, the cause of the state of mind of one individual is beyond the scope of observation by another.

This is because different objects produce different responses in different individuals. Our field of observation is limited to the symptoms, and cannot extend to the causes.

III.21

कायरूपसंयमात्तद्ग्राह्यशक्तिस्तम्भे चक्षुःप्रकाशासंप्रयोगेऽन्तर्धानम् ।

kāyarūpasaṁyamāttadgrāhyaśaktistambhe cakṣuḥprakāśāsaṁprayoge'ntardhānam

The physical features of one individual are distinguishable because they are different from their surroundings, in the same way as a white patch is obvious on a black wall, but a black patch is not.

Saṁyama on the relationship between the features of the body and what affects them, can give one the means to merge with one's surroundings in such a way that one's form is indistinguishable.

This is comparable to the camouflage principles employed by chameleons and many other animals. Thus, an experienced stalker can merge his human form with the environment, however featureless it is, by developing an acute awareness of what it is that differentiates him from his environment and minimizing its effects by the careful placing, moving and shaping of his human form.

III.22

सोपक्रमं निरुपक्रमं च कर्म तत्संयमादपरान्तज्ञानमरिष्टेभ्यो वा ।

sopakramaṁ nirupakramaṁ ca karma tatsaṁyamādaparāntajñānamariṣṭebhyo va

All actions are influenced by the purpose of the action, the state of mind of the actor, the clarity at our disposal and the circumstances.

The results of actions may be immediate or delayed. ***Saṁyama*** *on this can give one the ability to predict the course of future actions and even one's own death.*

III.23

मैत्र्यादिषु बलानि ।

maitryādiṣu balāni

Different qualities such as friendliness, compassion and contentment can be enquired into through ***saṁyama****. Thus, one can learn how to strengthen a chosen quality.*

In the same way, specific physical and mental skills can be obtained.

III.24

बलेषु हस्तिबलादीनि ।

baleṣu hastibalādīni

For example,

Saṁyama *on the physical strength of an elephant can give one the strength of an elephant*

This does not, of course, mean that we can acquire the same strength as an elephant – but we can acquire comparable strength proportionate to the limits of the human form.

III.25

प्रवृत्त्यालोकन्यासात्सूक्ष्मव्यवहितविप्रकृष्टज्ञानम् ।

pravṛttyālokanyāsātsūkṣmavyavahitaviprakṛṣṭajñānam

Directing the mind to the life force itself, and through saṁyama, sustaining that direction, results in the ability to observe fine subtleties and understand what is preventing deep observation.

In the absence of such fine abilities, our observation is distinctly limited.

III.26

भुवनज्ञानं सूर्ये संयमात् ।

bhuvanajñānaṁ sūrye saṁyamāt

Saṁyama can be directed towards the cosmos. A few examples follow.

Saṁyama on the sun gives wide knowledge of the planetary systems and the cosmic regions.

III.27

चन्द्रे ताराव्यूहज्ञानम् ।

candre tārāvyūhajñānam

Saṁyama on the moon gives a thorough knowledge of the positions of the stars at different times.

Observation of the different phases of the moon, its eclipses and the path on which it travels, takes us all over the sky and thus encompasses all the visible stars and their constellations.

III.28

ध्रुवे तद्गतिज्ञानम् ।

dhruve tadgatijñānam

For us on earth, everything seems to revolve around Polaris, the North Star. Thus,

Saṁyama on Polaris gives knowledge about the relative movements of the stars.

III.29

नाभिचक्रे कायव्यूहज्ञानम् ।

nābhicakre kāyavyūhajñānam

Even different parts of the body can be the objects of *Saṁyama*.

Saṁyama on the navel gives knowledge about the different organs of the body and their dispositions.

By virtue of its location in the mid-abdomen around which so many vital organs are found, as well as it being the channel through which the body received its vital needs while it was in the womb, the navel is considered the seat of some bodily forces.

III.30

कण्ठकूपे क्षुत्पिपासानिवृत्तिः ।

kaṇṭhakūpe kṣutpipāsānivṛttiḥ

Using the throat as the point of enquiry for Saṁyama provides an understanding of thirst and hunger. This enables one to control extreme symptoms.

Like the navel, the throat is a vital area. Our appetite for certain foods, hunger and thirst are all felt there.

III.31

कूर्मनाड्यां स्थैर्यम् ।

kūrmanāḍyāṁ sthairyam

Saṁyama on the chest area and enquiry into the sensations felt there in different physical and mental states gives one the means to remain stable and calm even in very stressful situations.

Many of the symptoms of stress and anxiety are felt in the chest area. Physical posture can be affected by mental state. For instance, a permanent stoop can be the result of a lack of self confidence.

III.32

मूर्धज्योतिषि सिद्धदर्शनम् ।

mūrdhajyotiṣi siddhadarśanam

Saṁyama on the source of high intelligence in an individual develops supernormal capabilities.

Through this, we may receive support and greater vision from the divine forces and consequently,

III.33

प्रातिभाद्वा सर्वम् ।

prātibhādvā sarvam

Anything can be understood. With each attempt, fresh and spontaneous understanding arises.

III.34

हृदये चित्तसंवित् ।

hrdaye cittasaṁvit

The heart is considered to be the seat of the mind.

Saṁyama on the heart will definitely reveal the qualities of the mind.

It is only when we are quiet and calm that this is possible. We cannot see the colour of the water in the lake if the lake is turbulent.

III.35

सत्त्वपुरुषयोरत्यन्तासंकीर्णयोः प्रत्ययाविशेषो भोगः परार्थत्वात्स्वार्थसंयमात्पुरुषज्ञानम् ।

sattvapuruṣayoratyantāsaṁkīrṇayoḥ pratyayāviśeṣo bhogaḥ parārthatvātsvārthasaṁyamātpuruṣajñānam

The mind, which is subject to change, and the Perceiver, which is not, are in proximity but are of distinct and different characters. When the mind is directed externally and acts mechanically towards objects there is either pleasure or pain. However, when at the appropriate time, an individual begins enquiry into the very nature of the link between the Perceiver and perception, the mind is disconnected from external objects and there arises the understanding of the Perceiver itself.

Under the influence of external stimuli, the mind is a mechanical instrument. The results can be unpleasant. This happens inspite of the central force of the Perceiver. However good the eye, if the glass is clouded, the object is blurred. Through *saṁyama*, enquiry and the practice of Yoga on the basis of *sūtra* II – 1, we can look into the mechanics of mental activity. Our minds gradually rise to a level where they can be disconnected from external objectives. In this silent moment, the understanding of the very source of perception is apparent.

III.36

ततः प्रातिभश्रावणवेदनादर्शास्वादवार्ता जायन्ते ।

tataḥ prātibhaśrāvaṇavedanādarśāsvādavārtā jāyante

What are the consequences of such a moment?

Then, one begins to acquire extraordinary capacities.

III.37

ते समाधावुपसर्गा व्युत्थाने सिद्धयः ।

te samādhāvupasargā vyutthāne siddhayaḥ

But the mind is like a double edged sword. These special faculties, acquired through *saṁyama*, may produce an illusion of freedom as opposed to the highest state, which is free from error.

*For an individual who may revert to a state of distraction, this extraordinary knowledge and the capabilities acquired through **saṁyama** are worth possessing. But, for one who seeks nothing less than a sustained state of Yoga, the results of **saṁyama** are obstacles in themselves.*

Incidental benefits along the way should not be confused with the eventual goal. However pleasurable our experiences are as we travel on a journey, they cannot be substitutes for our chosen destination. For example, on our way to snow capped peaks, we settle down by the shore of a lake to watch the beautiful swans, forgetting forever our original destination.

Having warned us about the limitations of *saṁyama*, *Patañjali* continues with other possibilities for it.

III.38

बन्धकारणशैथिल्यात्प्रचारसंवेदनाच्च चित्तस्य परशरीरावेशः ।

bandhakāraṇaśaithilyātpracārasaṁvedanācca cittasya paraśarīrāveśaḥ

The mind is a storehouse of experiences, which are distinct for each individual. In addition, its function is limited to the individual to whom it belongs. Thus, the mind becomes an isolated fortress, resisting all entry.

By enquiring into the cause of this rigid situation binding the mind to the individual, and examining the means of relaxing this rigidity, there is great potential for an individual to reach beyond the confines of himself.

The mind must have the ability to see the results of past actions which prevent clear perception. Through the systematic practice of *prāṇāyāma* and other disciplines, the range of mental activity can be extended to influence others. A teacher who seeks to transform a stupid or confused student must have this capacity.

III.39

उदानजयाज्जलपङ्ककण्टकादिष्वसङ्ग उत्क्रान्तिश्च ।

udānajayājjalapaṅkakaṇṭakādiṣvasaṅga utkrāntiśca

Physical pain is closely linked to the mind. A child completely absorbed in play may not be aware of hunger. But, later he may cry violently for food. Physical manifestations of sensations like pain are linked to the mind through vital forces that run through the body. These forces can be directed by certain practices like *prāṇāyāma* and different effects can be produced by specific modifications.

By mastering the forces that transmit sensations from the body to the mind, it is possible to master the external stimuli. For instance, one can tolerate water of any temperature or the effects of thorns, or one can walk on unstable surfaces and even feel as light as a balloon.

Cold, heat, sharp thorns - all these have relative effects. A summer in the Arctic may still feel wintery for someone used to the Tropics and someone used to the Arctic may find a Tropical winter unbearably hot. A farm worker in India may find walking through a paddy field as comfortable as a New Yorker finds walking on a concrete pavement.

III.40

समानजयाज्ज्वलनम् ।

samānajayājjvalanam

The life forces, (*prāṇa*) have different roles and differing areas of activity. For example *samāna* is responsible for digestion. It is based in the navel area.

*By mastering **samāna**, one can experience sensations of excessive heat.*

Digestion occurs when the gastric juices process the food that enters the stomach. If *samāna* is stimulated, the feeling of heat increases. The *prāṇāyāma* technique which emphasizes retention of breath after inhalation is suggested. Other techniques can also be considered.

III.41

श्रोत्राकाशयोः संबन्धसंयमाद्दिव्यं श्रोत्रम् ।

śrotrākāśayoḥ saṁbandhasaṁyamāddivyaṁ śrotram

We know that sound travels through space.

***Saṁyama** on the relationship between the sense of hearing and space develops an extraordinary sense of hearing.*

III.42

कायाकाशयोः संबन्धसंयमाल्लघुतूलसमापत्तेश्चाकाशगमनम् ।

kāyākāśayoḥ saṁbandhasaṁyamāllaghutūla-samāpatteścākāśagamanam

Man has long been interested in the relationship between physical objects and space. Why is it that birds can fly but a stone falls when thrown up?

*By doing **Saṁyama** on the relationship between the body and space, and examining the properties of objects that can float, such as cotton fluff, the knowledge to move about in space can be achieved.*

Again, this does not mean that we can learn how to physically float, but we can acquire an understanding of what it is to float. In the same way, the properties of a cotton seed prevent it from floating, but the same seed when changed to cotton fluff floats easily.

III.43

बहिरकल्पिता वृत्तिर्महाविदेहा ततः प्रकाशावरणक्षयः ।

bahirakalpitā vṛttirmahāvidehā tataḥ prakāśāvaraṇakṣayaḥ

The mind influences our perception through memory, imagination and other characteristics such as heaviness. But, the same mind can be altered to a state in which it does not colour the perception of an object. When this happens, our perception of an object is correct. Further, it is possible to completely withold the mind from perception of an object, no matter how attractive and tempting it might be.

By examining these phenomena and developing conditions when the mind does not confuse perception, there arises an extraordinary faculty with which one can probe other minds. In addition, the clouds that obscure correct perception are minimized.

Such developments are only possible in stages. The obscuring clouds are the obstacles described in *sūtra* II – 3.

III.44

स्थूलस्वरूपसूक्ष्मान्वयार्थवत्त्वसंयमाद्भूतजयः ।

***sthūlasvarūpasūkṣmānvayārthavattva-
saṁyamādbhūtajayaḥ***

Saṁyama on the origin of matter in all its forms, appearances and uses can develop into mastery of the elements.

Matter consists of elements in different forms but which are mutually related. Each element has a distinct existence. They comprise the body as well as things outside the body. And their characteristics change. They form the very basis of the objects we perceive, and if we are ignorant of their nature, we face problems.

III.45

ततोऽणिमादिप्रादुर्भावः कायसंपत्तद्धर्मानभिघातश्च ।

tato'ṇimādiprādurbhāvaḥ kāyasaṁpattaddharmānabhighātaśca

Thus,

When the elements are mastered, one is no longer disturbed by them. The body reaches perfection and extraordinary capabilities become possible.

These capabilities include the ability to modify our bodies to great heaviness, great lightness, etc.

III.46

रूपलावण्यबलवज्रसंहननत्वानि कायसंपत् ।

rūpalāvaṇyabalavajrasaṁhananatvāni kāyasaṁpat

Perfection in the body means good features, attractiveness to others, physical firmness and unusual physical strength.

III.47

ग्रहणस्वरूपास्मितान्वयार्थवत्त्वसंयमादिन्द्रियजयः ।

grahaṇasvarūpāsmitānvayārthavattvasaṁyamādindriyajayaḥ

Mastery over the senses is achieved through ***saṁyama*** *on the ability of the senses to observe their respective objects, how such objects are understood, how the individual identifies with the object, how the object, the senses, the mind and the Perceiver are interrelated and what results from such perception.*

The senses, the object and the mind have to be interlinked for an observation to materialize. This is possible because of the power of the Perceiver, as well as the power of the mind and the senses to register the object. In addition, the three common characteristics possessed by the mind, the senses and the object in different combinations (i.e. heaviness, activity and clarity) assist perception as much as they affect perception.

III.48

ततो मनोजवित्वं विकरणभावः प्रधानजयश्च ।

tato manojavitvaṁ vikaraṇabhāvaḥ pradhānajayaśca

Then, the responses of the senses will be as swift as that of the mind. They will perceive acutely and the individual will have the capacity to influence the characteristics of the elements.

Through this *saṁyama,* the changes that the elements undergo can be controlled at will. We gain the necessary knowledge to determine such changes, in the same way that a chemist can break down sea water into its component chemicals.

III.49

सत्त्वपुरुषान्यताख्यातिमात्रस्य सर्वभावाधिष्ठातृत्वं सर्वज्ञातृत्वं च ।

sattvapuruṣānyatākhyātimātrasya sarvabhāvādhiṣṭhātṛtvaṁ sarvajñātṛtvaṁ ca

When there is clear understanding of the difference between the Perceiver and the mind, all the various states of mind and what affects them become known. Then, the mind becomes a perfect instrument for the flawless perception of all that needs to be known.

III.50

तद्वैराग्यादपि दोषबीजक्षये कैवल्यम् ।

tadvairāgyādapi doṣabījakṣaye kaivalyam

These extraordinary capabilities that can be gained through *saṁyama* should not be the final goal. In fact,

Freedom, the last goal of Yoga, is attained only when the desire to acquire extraordinary knowledge is rejected and the source of obstacles is completely controlled.

III.51

स्थान्युपनिमन्त्रणे सङ्गस्मयाकरणं पुनरनिष्टप्रसङ्गात् ।

sthānyupanimantraṇe saṅgasmayākaraṇaṁ punaraniṣṭaprasaṅgāt

Otherwise,

The temptation to accept the respectful status as a consequence of acquiring knowledge through saṁyama should be restrained. Else, one is led to the same unpleasant consequences that arise from all obstacles to Yoga.

These obstacles include false identity. When respect for high learning is given more importance than everlasting freedom from the painful consequences of our actions, a fall is certain.

III.52

क्षणतत्क्रमयोः संयमाद्विवेकजं ज्ञानम् ।

kṣaṇatatkramayoḥ saṁyamādvivekajaṁ jñānam

Saṁyama on time and its sequence brings about absolute clarity.

Clarity is the ability to see distinctly the difference between one object and another and to see each object in its totality without impediments. Time is relative. It exists by comparison of one moment with another. A unit of time is in fact a representation of change. Change is the replacement of one characteristic by another. This link between time and change is what needs to be examined in this *saṁyama*.

III.53

जातिलक्षणदेशैरन्यतानवच्छेदात्तुल्ययोस्ततः प्रतिपत्तिः ।

jātilakṣaṇadeśairanyatānavacchedāttulyayostataḥ pratipattiḥ

This clarity makes it possible to distinguish objects even when the distinction is not apparently clear. Apparent similarity should not deter one from the distinct perception of a chosen object.

III.54

तारकं सर्वविषयं सर्वथाविषयमक्रमं चेति विवेकजं ज्ञानम् ।

tārakaṁ sarvaviṣayaṁ sarvathāviṣayaṁakramaṁ ceti vivekajaṁ jñānam

Further,

Such clarity is not exclusive of any object, any particular situation or any moment. It is not the result of sequential logic. It is immediate, spontaneous and total.

III.55

सत्त्वपुरुषयोः शुद्धिसाम्ये कैवल्यम् ।

sattvapuruṣayoḥ śuddhisāmye kaivalyam

What is freedom ?

Freedom is when the mind has complete identity with the Perceiver.

And nothing less. Then, the mind has no colour or features of its own.

Chapter 4

कैवल्यपादः

Kaivalyapādaḥ

In this, the final chapter of the *Yoga Sūtra-s*, *Kaivalyapādaḥ*, *Patañjali* presents the possibilities for a person with a highly refined mind. The mind is basically a servant and not a master. If the mind is allowed to play the role of master, whatever the achievements of the individual, there are bound to be problems and serenity will be beyond that individual's reach.

IV.1

जन्मौषधिमन्त्रतपःसमाधिजाः सिद्धयः ।

janmauṣadhimantratapaḥsamādhijāḥ siddhayaḥ

Exceptional mental capabilities may be achieved through genetic inheritance, the use of herbs as prescribed in the sacred texts, recitation of incantations, rigorous austerities and through that state of mind which remains one with its object without distractions (samādhi).

Some people are born with extraordinary capabilities. The sacred texts describe various rituals whereby the taking of herbal preparations in a prescribed way can change the person's personality. Different types of incantations, appropriately initiated by competent teachers can bring about positive changes.

Ancient scriptures record the great achievements of those who went through severe austerities. Finally, there are the possibilities for those who gradually change their minds from a state of distraction to one of sustained direction. These are mentioned in abundance in the third chapter and elsewhere. Whether any particular one of these alternatives is to be preferred will be examined in *sūtra-s* IV – 6, 7 and 8.

IV.2

जात्यन्तरपरिणामः प्रकृत्यापूरात् ।

jātyantarapariṇāmaḥ prakṛtyāpūrāt

How does the change resulting in the appearance of exceptional and supernormal possibilities come about?

Change from one set of characteristics to another is essentially an adjustment of the basic qualities of matter.

All that we perceive, including the mind, have three basic qualities - clarity, activity and heaviness. Different characteristics arise at different times as a result of different combinations of these three qualities. It is one of the changes in the characteristics of the mind that results in the supernormal capabilities that *Patañjali* speaks about in *sūtra* IV – 1.

IV.3

निमित्तमप्रयोजकं प्रकृतीनां वरणभेदस्तु ततः क्षेत्रिकवत् ।

nimittamaprayojakaṁ prakṛtīnāṁ varaṇabhedastu tataḥ kṣetrikavat

How can change in the characteristics of matter or mind be achieved? By profound intelligence.

But, such intelligence can only remove obstacles that obstruct certain changes. Its role is no more than that of a farmer who cuts a dam to allow water to flow into the field where it is needed.

This profound intelligence is the ability to perceive the role of the basic qualities in producing different characteristics. For example, the farmer who knows his field and the requirements of his crop will adjust the flow of the water to achieve the best yield. On the other hand, an ignorant novice who embarks on farming will fail in spite of having potentially good soil, water, climate and equipment.

IV.4

निर्माणचित्तान्यस्मितामात्रात् ।

nirmāṇacittānyasmitāmātrāt

What are the possibilities for someone with supernormal capabilities?

With exceptional mental faculties, an individual can influence the mental states of other beings.

IV.5

प्रवृत्तिभेदे प्रयोजकं चित्तमेकमनेकेषाम् ।

pravṛttibhede prayojakaṁ cittamekamanekeṣām

Are these influences consistent or variable?

This influence also depends on the state of the recipient.

How receptive is the person? What capabilities does he have? What does he lack? This decides the outcome of the influence of another. The same rain can relieve a drought striken farmer, worry a mother with inadequate shelter for her child and have no effect on the open ocean.

IV.6

तत्र ध्यानजमनाशयम् ।

tatra dhyānajamanāśayam

Is it only the state of the recipient that decides the final outcome of the effect on a person?

Influence on another by one whose mind is in a state of ***dhyāna*** *can never increase anxiety or other obstacles. In fact, they are reduced.*

Those who have reached this state of *dhyāna* through the gradual elimination of obstacles (see II – 3) are not blind to the conditions of human suffering. They know where the shoe pinches.

IV.7

कर्माशुक्लाकृष्णं योगिनस्त्रिविधमितरेषाम् ।

karmāśuklākṛṣṇaṁ yoginastrividhamitareṣām

And they act without any motivation, while others who also have exceptional capabilities act with some motivation or other.

In *sūtra* IV – 1, *Patañjali* lists the different means of achieving an exceptional or supernormal state of mind. Of them all, only those who have reached the state of Yoga in the correct way and through it have reached the highest state of clarity and detachment can be beyond motivation. They are naturally and unambiguously concerned. Therefore, they can help others to emulate their living examples. Others may appear to be in a state of Yoga, but their clarity and degree of detachment is not as complete and everlasting. Besides, they may be unaware of the limitations of man to follow their advice.

IV.8

ततस्तद्विपाकानुगुणानामेवाभिव्यक्तिर्वासनानाम् ।

tatastadvipākānuguṇānāmevābhivyaktirvāsanānām

How can these differences exist?

Since the tendency of the mind to act on the basis of obstacles, such as misapprehension, has not been erased, these obstacles will surface in the future and produce unpleasant consequences.

Only the practices described in earlier chapters to reduce and render the five obstacles ineffective can guarantee the end of these tendencies. Genetic inheritance, the use of herbs and other means cannot be as effective.

IV.9

जातिदेशकालव्यवहितानामप्यानन्तर्यं

स्मृतिसंस्कारयोरेकरूपत्वात् ।

jātideśakālavyavahitānāmapyānantaryaṁ smṛtisaṁskārayorekarūpatvāt

In addition,

Memory and latent impressions are strongly linked. This link remains even if there is an interval of time, place or context between similar actions.

This link between impressions and memory is an important contribution to most of our actions and their consequences.

IV.10

तासामनादित्वं चाशिषो नित्यत्वात् ।

tāsāmanāditvaṁ cāśiṣo nityatvāt

What is the origin of those impressions that influence our actions unpleasantly?

There is a strong desire for immortality in all men at all times, Thus, these impressions cannot be ascribed to any particular time.

One of the strange but ever present states in all beings is the desire to live for ever. Even those in the presence of death everyday have this illogical desire. This is what inspires the instinct for self preservation in all of us.

IV.11

हेतुफलाश्रयालम्बनैः संगृहीतत्वादेषामभावे तदभावः ।

hetuphalāśrayālambanaiḥ saṁgṛhītatvādesāmabhāve tadabhāvaḥ

Is there absolutely no hope at all of ending the effect of these undesirable impressions?

These tendencies are both maintained and sustained by misapprehensions, external stimuli, attachment to the fruits of actions and the quality of mind that promotes hyperactivity. Reduction of these automatically makes the undersirable impressions ineffective.

Various ways of reducing and eliminating these protective obstacles by regulated practices have already been indicated. There are many ways, including the help given by God. For those who do not appreciate God, there are many other ways described in the first three chapters. Conversely, it can also be said that impressions free from the five obstacles are in turn maintained and sustained by a discriminating mind.

IV.12

अतीतानागतं स्वरूपतोऽस्त्यध्वभेदाद्धर्माणाम् ।

atītānāgataṁ svarūpato'styadhvabhedāddharmāṇām

Whatever will appear in the future or has appeared in the

past is essentially in a dormant state, What is past has not disappeared for ever.

The substance of what has disappeared as well as what may appear always exists. Whether or not they are evident depends upon the direction of change.

Patañjali again stresses that nothing can be annihilated. What is replaced in the process of change remains in a dormant state.

IV.13

ते व्यक्तसूक्ष्मा गुणात्मानः ।

te vyaktasūkṣmā guṇātmānaḥ

Whether or not particular characteristics appear, depends on the mutations of the three qualities.

These qualities are heaviness, activity and clarity. All apparent characteristics are just different combinations of these three basic qualities that comprise all things (*sūtra* II – 18).

IV.14

परिणामैकत्वाद्वस्तुतत्त्वम् ।

pariṇāmaikatvādvastutattvam

The characteristics of a substance at one moment in time is in fact a single change in these qualities.

Change itself is a continuous process based on many factors (*sūtra-s* III – 9 to III-12). The required change in objects and in the mind can be achieved by knowing the potential combinations of these three qualities and what can influence them. There are many possible examples such as that given in *sūtra* IV – 3. Food and the environment provide others.

IV.15

वस्तुसाम्ये चित्तभेदात्तयोर्विभक्तः पन्थाः ।

vastusāmye cittabhedāttayorvibhaktaḥ panthāḥ

But are the characteristics of an object that appear to one observer the real characteristics?

The characteristics of an object appear differently, depending upon the different mental states of the observer.

This applies to one observer with different states of mind at different times as well as to various observers with different states of mind observing the object at the same time. Thus, a Hindu temple is a place of worship to the devoted believer, an artistic monument to the tourist, a place of solicitation to the beggar and even a place of ridicule to an atheist.

IV.16

न चैकचित्ततन्त्रं चेद्वस्तु तदप्रमाणकं तदा किं स्यात् ।

na caikacittatantraṁ cedvastu tadapramāṇakaṁ tadā kiṁ syāt

Does this not raise doubts about the common reality of any object? Can an object simply exist in the imagination of a person without having an independent reality?

If the object were indeed the conception of a particular individual's mind, then in the absence of his perception, would it exist?

Patañjali asks a rhetorical question. The answer is obvious. The existence of an object cannot depend solely on any one person's imagination. A river does not stop flowing because no one is looking at it.

IV.17

तदुपरागापेक्षित्वाच्चित्तस्य वस्तु ज्ञाताज्ञातम् ।

taduparāgāpekṣitvāccittasya vastu jñātājñātam

On what does the perception of an object depend?

Whether an object is perceived or not depends on its accessibility as well as the individual's motivation.

The object must exist. It must be observable and it must motivate the observer and stimulate in him/her a desire to see it.

IV.18

सदा ज्ञाताश्चित्तवृत्तयस्तत्प्रभोः पुरुषस्यापरिणामित्वात् ।

sadā jñātāścittavṛttayastatprabhoḥ puruṣasyāpariṇāmitvāt

What is it that sees? Is it the mind?

Mental activities are always known to the Perceiver which is non-changing and the master of the mind.

The mind cannot function without the power of the Perceiver. The mind changes, the Perceiver does not. The mind has the quality of heaviness but not so the Perceiver. All mental activities are therefore, observed by the Perceiver.

IV.19

न तत्स्वाभासं दृश्यत्वात् ।

na tatsvābhāsaṁ dṛśyatvāt

In addition, the mind is a part of what is perceived and has no power of its own to perceive.

The mind is seen, through its activities, in the same way that external objects, the body and senses are seen. Its very existence is dependent upon the Perceiver.

IV.20

एकसमये चोभयानवधारणम् ।

ekasamaye cobhayānavadhāraṇam

Let us suppose the mind itself could function in two roles, as the fabricator of what is observed and as the observer.

The premise that the mind can play two roles is untenable because it cannot simultaneously fabricate and see what it fabricates.

An object existing independently of an observer can be perceived. However, the concept of the mind creating an object, and at the same time, observing that object, is impossible to maintain. Another agency, independent of the mind and the ability to perceive, is essential.

IV.21

चित्तान्तरदृश्ये बुद्धिबुद्धेरतिप्रसङ्गः स्मृतिसंकरश्च ।

cittāntaradṛśye buddhibuddheratiprasaṅgaḥ smṛtisaṁkaraśca

If we then postulate the concept of a succession of minds that exist momentarily to create images and in turn recognize and observe them,

In an individual with such a series of minds of momentary existence there would be disorder and the difficulty of maintaining consistency of memory.

What is suggested in *sūtra-s* IV – 20 and IV – 21 is that there must be an independent source of perception. The mind can of course, influence the perception of an object. This object has an existence independent of the source of perception. If we insist on the concept of the mind from moment to moment being the source, means and object of perception, we face problems in comprehending the possibility of one person remembering what he saw in the past, sharing what he has seen and reconciling the fact that one object seen by one person is not necessarily seen by another or in the same way.

IV.22

चितेरप्रतिसंक्रमायास्तदाकारापत्तौ स्वबुद्धिसंवेदनम् ।

citerapratisaṁkramāyāstadākārāpattau svabuddhisaṁvedanam

Is the role of the mind limited to helping us see external objects?

When the mind is not linked to external objects and it does not reflect an external form to the Perceiver, then it takes the form of the Perceiver itself.

When there are no external stimuli and interests to extrapolate, there are no impressions in the mind relating to them. Then the mind is in total contact with and identical to the Perceiver. Then, cognition of the Perceiver is possible. This cognition is not by the mind. This is related to the concept of freedom in *sūtra* III – 55. It is assumed that the heaviness that causes sleep is not in operation.

IV.23

द्रष्टृदृश्योपरक्तं चित्तं सर्वार्थम् ।

draṣṭṛdṛśyoparaktaṁ cittaṁ sarvārtham

Thus, the mind serves a dual purpose. It serves the Perceiver by presenting the external to it. It also reflects or presents the Perceiver to itself for its own enlightenment.

IV.24

तदसंख्येयवासनाभिश्चित्रमपि परार्थं संहत्यकारित्वात् ।

tadasaṁkhyeyavāsanābhiścitramapi parārthaṁ saṁhatyakāritvāt

The role of the mind in serving the Perceiver in every way is further reiterated.

Even though the mind has accumulated various impressions of different types, it is always at the disposal of the Perceiver. This is because the mind cannot function without the power of the Perceiver.

The mind has no purpose of its own. It cannot act on its own. See *sūtra* II – 21.

IV.25

विशेषदर्शिन आत्मभावभावनानिवृत्तिः ।

viśeṣadarśina ātmabhāvabhāvanānivṛttiḥ

Patañjali now suggests the qualities of one who has reached the highest state of clarity.

A person of extraordinary clarity is one who is free from the desire to know the nature of the Perceiver.

One has no curiosity to speculate on the Perceiver, the quality of the mind, the "Where-was-I? and "What-will-I-be?" queries because he has felt his true nature. Such persons have reached a level that is free from obstacles, (*sūtra* II – 3) because one of the products of obstacles is the question "Who am I" ?

IV.26

तदा विवेकनिम्नं कैवल्यप्राग्भारं चित्तम् ।

tadā vivekanimnaṁ kaivalyaprāgbhāraṁ cittam

And their clarity takes them to their only concern - to reach and remain in a state of freedom.

IV.27

तच्छिद्रेषु प्रत्ययान्तराणि संस्कारेभ्यः ।

tacchidreṣu pratyayāntarāṇi saṁskārebhyaḥ

Is such a person now beyond regression?

In the unlikely possibility of distraction from this aim, disturbing past impressions are able to surface.

Since our actions are influenced by such impressions, regression, unlikely as it may seen, is still possible.

IV.28

हानमेषां क्लेशवदुक्तम् ।

hānameṣāṁ kleśavaduktam

One must never accommodate even small errors because they are as detrimental as the five obstacles.

Even at such a refined state of being, help from a teacher, who can see us through, is essential. In the first chapter (*sūtra* I – 30) regression is considered to be one of the impediments to progress, and is as serious as disease and doubt.

IV.29

प्रसंख्यानेऽप्यकुसीदस्य सर्वथा
विवेकख्यातेर्धर्ममेघः समाधिः ।

prasaṁkhyāne'pyakusīdasya sarvathā
vivekakhyāterdharmameghaḥ samādhiḥ

When we have crosed the last hurdle

There arises a state of mind full of clarity concerning all things at all times. It is like a rainfall of pure clarity.

Life is full of contentment. Vision is never dimmed. The extraordinary capabilities are never misused.

IV.30

ततः क्लेशकर्मनिवृत्तिः ।

tataḥ kleśakarmanivṛttiḥ

This is indeed the state free from actions based on the five obstacles.

But it is not a life without action. It is a life devoid of errors and selfish interests.

IV.31

तदा सर्वावरणमलापेतस्य ज्ञानस्यानन्त्याज्ज्ञेयमल्पम् ।

tadā sarvāvaraṇamalāpetasya jñānasyānantyājjñeyamalpam

When the mind is free from the clouds that prevent perception, all is known. There is nothing left to be known.

The sun shines. All is evident. There is no need for artificial light.

IV.32

ततः कृतार्थानां परिणामक्रमसमाप्तिर्गुणानाम् ।

tataḥ kṛtārthānāṁ pariṇāmakramasamāptirguṇānām

With this highest potential at our disposal,

The three basic qualities cease to follow the sequence of alternating pain and pleasure.

With higher intelligence potential at our disposal, the objects of perception are in our control. Their mutations through the combination of the three qualities occur no more. We are able to influence them to serve our immediate needs, without ever producing or provoking regrettable actions. Changes in the mind, body and senses no longer create trouble.

IV.33

क्षणप्रतियोगी परिणामापरान्तनिर्ग्राह्यः क्रमः ।

kṣaṇapratiyogī pariṇāmāparāntanirgrāhyaḥ kramaḥ

What is a sequence?

A sequence is the replacement of one characteristic by another that follows it. This is linked to the moment. A replacement of characteristics is also the basis of a moment.

Moment, which is the basic unit of time, and sequence are related. The change in the characteristics of an object is their common basis. The sequence is affected by the changes. Therefore, time is essentially relative, in that it is the essential of change. The order of change is the variation in the characteristics that follow one after the other (see *sūtra-s* III – 15 and III – 52).

In the context of *sūtra* IV – 32, the changes that now arise in the objects of perception, follow a different sequence from those of the past when it was both unpredictable and liable to bring regrets. Now the individual can command the changes.

IV.34

पुरुषार्थशून्यानां गुणानां प्रतिप्रसवः
कैवल्यं स्वरूपप्रतिष्ठा वा चितिशक्तिरिति ।

puruṣārthaśūnyānāṁ guṇānāṁ pratiprasavaḥ kaivalyaṁ svarūpapratiṣṭhā vā citiśaktiriti

What is the final state of yoga?

When the highest purpose of life is achieved, the three basic qualities do not excite responses in the mind. That is freedom. In other words, the Perceiver is no longer coloured by the mind.

It is serenity in action as well as in inaction. There is no sense of obligation, whether to take responsibility or to reject it. The three qualities can no longer combine to disrupt the individual. He is fully conscious of his own state of pure clarity and the clarity remains at the highest level throughout his lifetime. The mind is a faithful servant to the master, the Perceiver.

Part - II

Yoga Sūtra-s
Text with Chant Notations

Yoga Sūtra-s with Chant Notations

In recent times, many people are interested in reciting the *Yoga Sūtra-s* of *Patañjali*. While an understanding of the *Sūtra-s* can be facilitated with the help of teachers and through books, actual recitation of the *Sūtra-s* requires notations. In this section, we present in a simplified manner, the *Yoga Sūtra-s* of *Patañjali* with the chant notations. The compound words in the *Sūtra-s* have been split to make recitation simpler for beginners. The *Sūtra-s* with chant notations are presented in Sanskrit as well as in the transliterated form, to benefit those who are unfamiliar with the Sanskrit script. The *Sūtra-s* have been presented as received from our teacher. However, in certain places to maintain consistency in the recitation of the *Sūtra-s* in the classical and simple versions, some liberties have been taken. We hope this will be excused.

Note – Hyphen indicates a pause during recitation. There are three accents (svara-s) or levels of pitch that fall on the vowels. These are :

Svarita – This is indicated by the absence of any mark above or below the syllables and is the primary reference note.

Udātta – This is indicated by a vertical line over the syllable and represents a pitch higher than the reference note.

Anudātta – This is indicated by a horizontal line placed beneath the syllable and represents a pitch lower than the reference note.

Nigādha - There is another special type of note known as *Nigādha* which can be defined as a delayed *Udātta*. It is represented by two parallel vertical lines placed above the syllable. The syllable is pronounced in *Svarita* first and then raised to a higher note one unit later.

समाधिपादः
Samādhipādaḥ

I-1 अथ - योगानुशासनम् ।

atha - yogānuśāsanam

I-2 योगः - चित्तवृत्तिनिरोधः ।

yogaḥ - cittavṛttinirodhaḥ

I-3 तदा - द्रष्टुः - स्वरूपे - अवस्थानम् ।

tadā - draṣṭuḥ - svarūpe - avāsthanam

I-4 वृत्तिसारूप्यम् - इतरत्र ।

vṛttisārūpyam - itaratra

I-5 वृत्तयः - पञ्चतय्यः - क्लिष्टाक्लिष्टाः ।

vṛttayaḥ - pañcatayyaḥ - kliṣṭākliṣṭāḥ

I-6 प्रमाण - विपर्यय - विकल्प - निद्रा - स्मृतयः ।

pramāṇa - viparyaya - vikalpa - nidrā - smṛtayaḥ

I-7 प्रत्यक्ष - अनुमान - आगमाः - प्रमाणानि ।

pratyakṣa - anumāna - āgamāḥ - pramāṇāni

I-8 विपर्ययो - मिथ्याज्ञानम् - अतद्रूपप्रतिष्ठम् ।

viparyayo - mithyājñānam - atadrūpapratiṣṭham

I-9 शब्दज्ञानानुपाती - वस्तुशून्यो - विकल्पः ।

śabdajñanānupātī - vastuśūnyo - vikalpaḥ

I-10 अभावप्रत्ययालम्बना - तमोवृत्तिर्निद्रा ।

abhāvapratyayālambanā - tamovṛttirnidrā

I-11 अनुभूतविषय - असंप्रमोषः - स्मृतिः ।

anubhūtaviṣaya - asaṁpramoṣaḥ - smṛtiḥ

I-12 अभ्यासवैराग्याभ्यां - तन्निरोधः ।

abhyāsavairāgyabhyāṁ - tannirodhaḥ

I-13 तत्र स्थितौ - यत्नोऽभ्यासः ।

tatra sthitau - yatno'bhyāsaḥ

I-14 स तु - दीर्घकाल - नैरन्तर्य - सत्कार - आदरा

आसेवितो - दृढभूमिः ।

sa tu - dīrghakāla - nairantarya - satkāra - ādarā -

āsevito - dṛḍhabhūmiḥ

I-15 दृष्टानुश्रविक - विषयवितृष्णस्य - वशीकारसंज्ञा -

वैराग्यम् ।

dṛṣṭānuśravika - viṣayavitṛṣṇasya -vaśīkārasaṁjñā -

vairāgyam

I-16 तत्परं - पुरुषख्यातेः - गुणवैतृष्ण्यम् ।

tatparaṁ - puruṣakhyāteḥ - guṇavaitṛṣṇyam

I-17 वितर्क - विचार - आनन्द - अस्मितारूप -

अनुगमात् - संप्रज्ञातः ।

vitarka - vicāra - ānanda - asmitārupa -

anugāmat - saṁprajñātaḥ

I-18 विरामप्रत्यय - अभ्यासपूर्वः - संस्कारशेषः - अन्यः ।

virāmapratyaya - abhyāsapūrvaḥ - saṁskāraśeṣaḥ - anyaḥ

I-19 भवप्रत्ययो - विदेहप्रकृतिलयानाम् ।

bhavapratyayo - videhaprakṛtilayānām

I-20 श्रद्धा - वीर्य - स्मृति - समाधिप्रज्ञा - पूर्वक इतरेषाम् ।

śraddhā - vīrya - smṛti - samādhiprajñā - pūrvaka itareṣām

I-21 तीव्रसंवेगानाम् - आसन्नः ।

tīvrasaṁvegānām - āsannaḥ

I-22 मृदु - मध्य - अधिमात्रत्वात् - ततोऽपि - विशेषः ।

mṛdu - madhya - adhimātratvāt - tato'pi - viśeṣaḥ

I-23 ईश्वर - प्रणिधानाद्वा ।

īśvara - praṇidhānādvā

I-24 क्लेश - कर्म - विपाक - आशयैः - अपरामृष्टः -

kleśa - karma - vipāka - āśayaiḥ - aparāmṛṣṭaḥ -

पुरुषविशेष ईश्वरः ।

puruṣaviśeṣa īśvaraḥ

I-25 तत्र - निरतिशयं - सर्वज्ञबीजम् ।

tatra - niratiśayaṁ - sarvajñabījam

I-26 स एष - पूर्वेषामपि गुरुः - कालेनानवच्छेदात् ।

sa eṣa - pūrveṣāmapi guruḥ - kālenānavacchedāt

I-27 तस्य - वाचकः - प्रणवः ।

tasya - vācakaḥ - praṇavaḥ

I-28 तज्जपः - तदर्थभावनम् ।

tajjapaḥ - tadarthabhāvanam

I-29 ततः - प्रत्यक्चेतनाधिगमः - अपि -

अन्तरायाभावश्च ।

tataḥ - pratyakcetanādhigamaḥ - api -

antarāyābhāvaśca

I-30 व्याधि - स्त्यान - संशय - प्रमाद - आलस्य -

अविरति - भ्रान्तिदर्शन - अलब्धभूमिकत्व -

अनवस्थितत्वानि - चित्तविक्षेपाः - ते -

अन्तरायाः ।

vyādhi - styāna - saṁśaya - pramāda - ālasya -

avirati - bhrāntidarśana - alabdhabhūmikatva -

anavasthitatvāni - cittavikṣepāḥ - te - antarāyāḥ

I-31 दुःख - दौर्मनस्य - अङ्गमेजयत्व -

श्वासप्रश्वासाः - विक्षेपसहभुवः ।

duḥkha - daurmanasya - aṅgamejayatva -

śvāsapraśvāsāḥ - vikṣepasahabhuvaḥ

I-32 तत्प्रतिषेधार्थम् - एकतत्त्वाभ्यासः ।

tatpratiṣedhārtham - ekatattvābhyāsaḥ

I-33 मैत्रीकरुणा - मुदितोपेक्षाणां - सुखदुःख -

पुण्यापुण्यविषयाणां - भावनातः - चित्तप्रसादनम् ।

maitrīkaruṇā - muditopekṣāṇāṁ - sukhaduḥkha

puṇyāpuṇyaviṣayāṇāṁ - bhāvanātaḥ - cittaprasādanam

I-34 प्रच्छर्दन - विधारणाभ्यां - वा - प्राणस्य ।

pracchardana - vidhāraṇābhyaṁ - vā - prāṇasya

I-35 विषयवती वा - प्रवृत्तिरुत्पन्ना - मनसः - स्थिति -

निबन्धिनी ।

viṣayavatī vā - pravṛttirutpannā - manasaḥ - sthiti -

nibandhinī

I-36 विशोका वा - ज्योतिष्मती ।

viśokā vā - jyotiṣmatī

I-37 वीतरागविषयं वा - चित्तम् ।

vītarāgaviṣayaṁ vā - cittam

I-38 स्वप्ननिद्रा - ज्ञानालम्बनं वा ।

svapnanidrā - jñānālambanaṁ vā

I-39 यथाभिमत - ध्यानाद्वा ।

yathābhimata - dhyānādvā

I-40 परमाणु - परममहत्त्वान्तः - अस्य वशीकारः ।

paramāṇu - paramamahattvāntaḥ - asya vaśīkāraḥ

I-41 क्षीणवृत्तेः - अभिजातस्येव मणेः - ग्रहीतृ - ग्रहण -
ग्राह्येषु - तत्स्थ तदञ्जनता - समापत्तिः ।

kṣīṇavṛtteḥ - abhijātasyeva maṇeḥ - grahītṛ - grahaṇa -
grāhyeṣu - tatstha tadañjanatā - samāpattiḥ

I-42 तत्र - शब्दार्थज्ञानविकल्पैः - संकीर्णा - सवितर्का -
समापत्तिः ।

tatra - śabdārthajñānavikalpaiḥ - saṃkīrna - savitarkā -
samāpattiḥ

I-43 स्मृतिपरिशुद्धौ - स्वरूपशून्येव - अर्थमात्रनिर्भासा - निर्वितर्का ।

smṛtipariśuddhau - svarūpaśūnyeva - arthamātranirbhāsā - nirvitarkā

I-44 एतयैव - सविचारा - निर्विचारा च - सूक्ष्मविषया - व्याख्याता ।

etayaiva - savicārā - nirvicārā ca - sūkṣmaviṣayā - vyākhyātā

I-45 सूक्ष्मविषयत्वं च - अलिङ्गपर्यवसानम् ।

sūkṣmaviṣayatvaṁ ca - aliṅgaparyavasānam

I-46 ता एव - सबीजः समाधिः ।

tā eva - sabījaḥ samādhiḥ

I-47 निर्विचारवैशारद्ये - अध्यात्मप्रसादः ।

nirvicāravaiśāradye - adhyātmaprasādaḥ

I-48 ऋतंभरा - तत्र प्रज्ञा ।

ṛtaṁbharā - tatra prajñā

I-49 श्रुतानुमानप्रज्ञाभ्याम् - अन्यविषया -

विशेषार्थत्वात् ।

śrutānumānaprajñābhyām - anyaviṣayā -

viśeṣārthatvāt

I-50 तज्जः संस्कारः - अन्यसंस्कारप्रतिबन्धी ।

tajjaḥ saṁskāraḥ - anyasaṁskārapratibandhī

I-51 तस्यापि निरोधे - सर्वनिरोधात् - निर्बीजः

समाधिः ।

tasyāpi nirodhe - sarvanirodhāt - nirbījaḥ samādhiḥ

साधनपादः
Sādhanapādaḥ

II-1 तपः - स्वाध्याय - ईश्वरप्रणिधानानि - क्रियायोगः ।

tapaḥ - svādhyāya - īśvarapraṇidhānāni - kriyāyogaḥ

II-2 समाधिभावनार्थः - क्लेश - तनूकरणार्थश्च ।

samādhibhāvanārthaḥ - kleśa - tanūkaraṇārthaśca

II-3 अविद्या - अस्मिता - राग - द्वेष - अभिनिवेशाः - क्लेशाः ।

avidyā - asmitā - rāga - dveṣa - abhiniveśāḥ - kleśāḥ

II-4 अविद्या क्षेत्रम् - उत्तरेषां - प्रसुप्त - तनु - विच्छिन्न - उदाराणाम् ।

avidyā kṣetram - uttareṣāṁ - prasupta - tanu - vicchinna - udārāṇām

II-5 अनित्य - अशुचि - दुःख - अनात्मसु - नित्य -

शुचि - सुख - आत्मख्यातिः - अविद्या ।

anitya - aśuci - duḥkha - anātmasu - nitya -

śuci - sukha - ātmakhyātiḥ - avidyā

II-6 दृग्दर्शनशक्त्योः - एकात्मता - इव - अस्मिता ।

dṛgdarśanaśaktyoḥ - ekātmatā - iva - asmitā

II-7 सुखानुशयी - रागः ।

sukhānuśayī - rāgaḥ

II-8 दुःखानुशयी - द्वेषः ।

duḥkhānuśayī - dveṣaḥ

II-9 स्वरसवाही - विदुषोऽपि - समारूढः - अभिनिवेशः ।

svarasavāhi - viduṣo'pi - samārūḍhaḥ - abhiniveśaḥ

II-10 ते - प्रतिप्रसवहेयाः - सूक्ष्माः ।

te - pratiprasavaheyāḥ - sūkṣmāḥ

II-11 ध्यानहेयाः - तद्वृत्तयः ।

dhyānaheyāḥ - tadvṛttayaḥ

II-12 क्लेशमूलः - कर्माशयो - दृष्टादृष्टजन्म - वेदनीयः ।

kleśamūlaḥ - karmāśayo - dṛṣṭādṛṣṭajanma - vedanīyaḥ

II-13 सति मूले - तद्विपाको - जात्यायुर्भोगाः ।

sati mūle - tadvipāko - jātyāyurbhogāḥ

II-14 ते - ह्लादपरितापफलाः - पुण्यापुण्यहेतुत्वात् ।

te - hlādaparitāpaphalāḥ - puṇyāpuṇyahetutvāt

II-15 परिणाम - ताप - संस्कारदुःखैः - गुणवृत्तिविरोधाच्च -

दुःखमेव सर्वं - विवेकिनः ।

pariṇāma - tāpa - saṁskāraduḥkhaiḥ - guṇavṛttivirodhācca -

duḥkhameva sarvaṁ - vivekinaḥ

II-16 हेयं - दुःखमनागतम् ।

heyaṁ - duḥkhamanāgatam

II-17 द्रष्टृदृश्ययोः - संयोगो - हेयहेतुः ।

draṣṭṛdṛśyayoḥ - saṁyogo - heyahetuḥ

II-18 प्रकाशक्रियास्थितिशीलं - भूतेन्द्रियात्मकं -
भोगापवर्गार्थं - दृश्यम् ।

prakāśakriyāsthitiśīlaṁ - bhūtendriyātmakaṁ -
bhogāpavargārthaṁ - dṛśyam

II-19 विशेषाविशेष - लिङ्गमात्रालिङ्गानि - गुणपर्वाणि ।

viśeṣāviśeṣa - liṅgamātrāliṅgāni - guṇaparvāṇi

II-20 द्रष्टा दृशिमात्रः - शुद्धोऽपि - प्रत्ययानुपश्यः ।

draṣṭā dṛśimātraḥ - śuddho'pi - pratyayānupaśyaḥ

II-21 तदर्थ एव - दृश्यस्य - आत्मा ।

tadartha eva - dṛśyasya - ātmā

II-22 कृतार्थं - प्रतिनष्टम् - अपि - अनष्टं -
तदन्यसाधारणत्वात् ।

kṛtārthaṁ - pratinaṣṭam - api - anaṣṭaṁ
tadanyasādhāraṇatvāt

II-23 स्वस्वामिशक्त्योः - स्वरूपोपलब्धिहेतुः - संयोगः ।

svasvāmiśaktyoḥ - svarūpopalabdhihetuḥ - saṁyogaḥ

II-24 तस्य हेतुः - अविद्या ।

tasya hetuḥ - avidyā

II-25 तदभावात् - संयोगाभावो - हानं - तद्दृशेः कैवल्यम् ।

tadabhāvāt - saṁyogābhāvo - hānaṁ - taddṛśeḥ kaivalyam

II-26 विवेकख्यातिः - अविप्लवा - हानोपायः ।

vivekakhyātiḥ - aviplavā - hānopāyaḥ

II-27 तस्य सप्तधा - प्रान्तभूमिः - प्रज्ञा ।

tasya saptadhā - prāntabhūmiḥ - prajñā

II-28 योगाङ्गानुष्ठानात् - अशुद्धिक्षये - ज्ञानदीप्तिः - आविवेकख्यातेः ।

yogāṅgānuṣṭhānāt - aśuddhikṣaye - jñānadīptiḥ - āvivekakhyāteḥ

II-29 यम - नियम - आसन - प्राणायाम - प्रत्याहार - धारणा - ध्यान - समाधयः - अष्टौ - अङ्गानि ।

yama - niyama - āsana - prāṇāyāma - pratyāhāra - dhāraṇā - dhyāna - samādhayaḥ - aṣṭau - aṅgāni

II-30 अहिंसा - सत्य - अस्तेय - ब्रह्मचर्य - अपरिग्रहाः - यमाः ।

ahiṁsā - satya - asteya - brahmacarya - aparigrahāḥ - yamāḥ

II-31 जाति - देश - काल - समय - अनवच्छिन्नाः -

सार्वभौमाः - महाव्रतम् ।

jāti - deśa - kāla - samaya - anavacchinnāḥ -

sārvabhaumāḥ - mahāvratam

II-32 शौच - संतोष - तपः - स्वाध्याय -

ईश्वरप्रणिधानानि - नियमाः ।

śauca - saṁtosa - tapaḥ - svādhyāya -

īśvarapraṇidhānāni - niyamāḥ

II-33 वितर्कबाधने - प्रतिपक्षभावनम् ।

vitarkabādhane - pratipakṣabhāvanam

II-34 वितर्काः - हिंसादयः - कृत - कारित -
अनुमोदिताः - लोभ - क्रोध - मोहपूर्वकाः -
मृदु - मध्य - अधिमात्राः - दुःख - अज्ञान -
अनन्तफलाः - इति प्रतिपक्षभावनम् ।

vitarkāḥ - hiṁsādayaḥ - kṛta - kārita -
anumoditāḥ - lobha - krodha - mohapūrvakāḥ -
mṛdu - madhya - adhimātrāḥ - duḥkhā - ajñāna -
anantaphalāḥ - iti pratipakṣabhāvanam

II-35 अहिंसाप्रतिष्ठायां - तत्सन्निधौ - वैरत्यागः ।

ahiṁsāpratiṣṭhāyāṁ - tatsannidhau - vairatyāgaḥ

II-36 सत्यप्रतिष्ठायां - क्रियाफल - आश्रयत्वम् ।

satyapratiṣṭhāyāṁ - kriyāphala - āśrayatvam

II-37 अस्तेयप्रतिष्ठायां - सर्वरत्न - उपस्थानम् ।

asteyapratiṣṭhāyāṁ - sarvaratna - upasthānam

II-38 ब्रह्मचर्यप्रतिष्ठायां - वीर्यलाभः ।

brahmacaryapratiṣṭhāyāṁ - vīryalābhaḥ

II-39 अपरिग्रहस्थैर्ये - जन्मकथंता - संबोधः ।

aparigrahasthairye - janmakathaṁtā - saṁbodhaḥ

II-40 शौचात् - स्वाङ्गजुगुप्सा - परैरसंसर्गः ।

śaucāt - svāṅgajugupsā - parairasaṁsargaḥ

II-41 सत्त्वशुद्धि - सौमनस्य - ऐकाग्र्य - इन्द्रियजय - आत्मदर्शन - योग्यत्वानि च ।

sattvaśuddhi - saumanasya - aikāgrya - indriyajaya - ātmadarśana - yogyatvāni ca

II-42 संतोषात् - अनुत्तमः - सुखलाभः ।

saṁtoṣāt - anuttamaḥ - sukhalābhaḥ

II-43 कायेन्द्रियसिद्धिः - अशुद्धिक्षयात् - तपसः ।

kāyendriyasiddhiḥ - aśuddhikṣayāt - tapasaḥ

II-44 स्वाध्यायात् - इष्टदेवतासंप्रयोगः ।

svādhyāyāt - iṣṭadevatāsaṁprayogaḥ

II-45 समाधिसिद्धिः - ईश्वरप्रणिधानात् ।

samādhisiddhiḥ - īśvarapraṇidhānāt

II-46 स्थिरसुखमासनम् ।

sthirasukhamāsanam

II-47 प्रयत्नशैथिल्य - अनन्तसमापत्तिभ्याम् ।

prayatnaśaithilya - anantasamāpattibhyām

II-48 ततो - द्वन्द्वानभिघातः ।

tato - dvaṅdvānabhighātaḥ

II-49 तस्मिन्सति - श्वासप्रश्वासयोः - गतिविच्छेदः
प्राणायामः ।

tasminsati - śvāsapraśvāsayoḥ - gativicchedaḥ
prāṇāyāmaḥ

II-50 बाह्य - आभ्यन्तर - स्तम्भवृत्तिः - देश - काल -

संख्याभिः - परिदृष्टो - दीर्घसूक्ष्मः ।

bāhya - ābhyantara - stambhavṛttiḥ - deśa - kāla -

saṁkhyābhiḥ - paridṛṣṭo - dīrghasūkṣmaḥ

II-51 बाह्य - आभ्यन्तर - विषयाक्षेपी - चतुर्थः ।

bāhya - ābhyantara - viṣayākṣepī - caturthaḥ

II-52 ततः - क्षीयते - प्रकाशावरणम् ।

tataḥ - kṣīyate - prakāśāvaraṇam

II-53 धारणासु च - योग्यता मनसः ।

dhāraṇāsu ca - yogyatā manasaḥ

II-54 स्वविषय - असंप्रयोगे - चित्तस्य - स्वरूपानुकार

इव - इन्द्रियाणां प्रत्याहारः ।

svaviṣaya - asaṁprayoge - cittasya - svarūpānukāra

iva - indriyāṇāṁ pratyāhāraḥ

II-55 ततः - परमा वश्यता - इन्द्रियाणाम् ।

tataḥ - paramā vaśyatā - indriyāṇām

विभूतिपादः
Vibhūtipādaḥ

III-1 देशबन्धः - चित्तस्य धारणा ।

deśabandhaḥ - cittasya dhāraṇā

III-2 तत्र - प्रत्ययैकतानता - ध्यानम् ।

tatra - pratyayaikatānatā - dhyānam

III-3 तदेव - अर्थमात्रनिर्भासं - स्वरूपशून्यमिव - समाधिः ।

tadeva - arthamātranirbhāsaṁ - svarūpaśūnyamiva - samādhiḥ

III-4 त्रयमेकत्र - संयमः ।

trayamekatra - saṁyamaḥ

III-5 तज्जयात् - प्रज्ञालोकः ।

tajjayāt - prajñālokaḥ

III-6 तस्य भूमिषु - विनियोगः ।

tasya bhūmiṣu - viniyogaḥ

III-7 त्रयमन्तरङ्गं - पूर्वेभ्यः ।

trayamantaraṅgaṁ - pūrvebhyaḥ

III-8 तदपि बहिरङ्गं - निर्बीजस्य ।

tadapi bahiraṅgaṁ - nirbījasya

III-9 व्युत्थाननिरोधसंस्कारयोः - अभिभवप्रादुर्भावौ - निरोधक्षणचित्तान्वयो - निरोधपरिणामः ।

vyutthānanirodhasaṁskārayoḥ -
abhibhavaprādurbhāvau -
nirodhakṣaṇacittānvayo - nirodhapariṇāmaḥ

III-10 तस्य - प्रशान्तवाहिता - संस्कारात् ।

tasya - praśāntavāhitā - saṁskārāt

III-11 सर्वार्थतैकाग्रतयोः - क्षयोदयौ - चित्तस्य - समाधिपरिणामः ।

sarvārthataikāgratayoḥ - kṣayodayau - cittasya - samādhipariṇāmaḥ

III-12 ततः - पुनः - शान्तोदितौ - तुल्यप्रत्ययौ - चित्तस्य - एकाग्रतापरिणामः ।

tataḥ - punaḥ - śāntoditau - tulyapratyayau - cittasya - ekāgratāpariṇāmaḥ

III-13 एतेन - भूतेन्द्रियेषु - धर्म - लक्षण - अवस्था - परिणामाः - व्याख्याताः ।

etena - bhūtendriyeṣu - dharma - lakṣaṇa - avasthā - pariṇāmāḥ - vyākhyātāḥ

III-14 शान्त - उदित - अव्यपदेश्य - धर्मानुपाती - धर्मी ।

śānta - udita - avyapadeśya - dharmānupātī - dharmī

III-15 क्रमान्यत्वं - परिणामान्यत्वे हेतुः ।

kramānyatvaṁ - pariṇāmānyatve hetuḥ

III-16 परिणामत्रयसंयमात् - अतीतानागतज्ञानम् ।

pariṇāmātrayasaṁyamāt - atītānāgatajñānam

III-17 शब्दार्थप्रत्ययानाम् - इतरेतराध्यासात् - संकरः

तत्प्रविभागसंयमात् - सर्वभूतरुतज्ञानम् ।

śabdārthapratyayānām - itaretarādhyāsāt - saṁkaraḥ -

tatpravibhāgasaṁyamāt - sarvabhūtarutajñānam

III-18 संस्कारसाक्षात्करणात् - पूर्वजातिज्ञानम् ।

saṁskārasākṣātkaraṇāt - pūrvajātijñānam

III-19 प्रत्ययस्य - परचित्तज्ञानम् ।

pratyayasya - paracittajñānam

III-20 न च - तत्सालम्बनं - तस्याविषयीभूतत्वात् ।

na ca - tatsālambanaṁ - tasyāviṣayībhūtatvāt

III-21 कायरूपसंयमात् - तद्ग्राह्यशक्तिस्तम्भे - चक्षुः -
प्रकाशासंप्रयोगे - अन्तर्धानम् ।

kāyarūpasaṁyamāt - tadgrāhyaśaktistambhe - cakṣuḥ -
prakāśāsaṁprayoge - antardhānam

III-22 सोपक्रमं - निरुपक्रमं च कर्म - तत्संयमात् -
अपरान्तज्ञानम् - अरिष्टेभ्यो वा ।

sopakramaṁ - nirupakramaṁ ca karma - tatsaṁyamāt -
aparāntajñānam - ariṣṭebhyo va

III-23 मैत्र्यादिषु - बलानि ।

maitryādiṣu - balāni

III-24 बलेषु - हस्तिबलादीनि ।

baleṣu - hastibalādīni

III-25 प्रवृत्त्यालोकन्यासात् - सूक्ष्म - व्यवहित - विप्रकृष्टज्ञानम् ।

pravṛttyālokanyāsāt - sūkṣma - vyavahita - viprakṛṣṭajñānam

III-26 भुवनज्ञानं - सूर्ये संयमात् ।

bhuvanajñānaṁ - sūrye saṁyamāt

III-27 चन्द्रे - ताराव्यूहज्ञानम् ।

candre - tārāvyūhajñānam

III-28 ध्रुवे - तद्गतिज्ञानम् ।

dhruve - tadgatijñānam

III-29 नाभिचक्रे - कायव्यूहज्ञानम् ।

nābhicakre - kāyavyūhajñānam

III-30 कण्ठकूपे - क्षुत्पिपासानिवृत्तिः ।

kaṅṭhakūpe - kṣutpipāsānivṛttiḥ

III-31 कूर्मनाड्यां - स्थैर्यम् ।

kūrmanāḍyāṁ - sthairyam

III-32 मूर्धज्योतिषि - सिद्धदर्शनम् ।

mūrdhajyotiṣi - siddhadarśanam

III-33 प्रातिभाद्वा - सर्वम् ।

prātibhādvā - sarvam

III-34 हृदये - चित्तसंवित् ।

hrdaye - cittasaṁvit

III-35 सत्त्वपुरुषयोः - अत्यन्तासंकीर्णयोः - प्रत्ययाविशेषो भोगः - परार्थत्वात् - स्वार्थसंयमात् - पुरुषज्ञानम् ।

sattvapuruṣayoḥ - atyantāsaṁkīrṇayoḥ - pratyayāviśeṣo bhogaḥ - parārthatvāt - svārthasaṁyamāt - puruṣajñānam

III-36 ततः - प्रातिभ - श्रावण - वेदन - आदर्श - आस्वादवार्ता - जायन्ते ।

tataḥ - prātibha - śrāvaṇa - vedana - ādarśa - āsvādavārtā - jāyante

III-37 ते समाधावुपसर्गाः - व्युत्थाने सिद्धयः ।

te samādhāvupasargāḥ - vyutthāne siddhayaḥ

III-38 बन्धकारणशैथिल्यात् - प्रचारसंवेदनाच्च -

चित्तस्य - परशरीरावेशः ।

bandhakāraṇaśaithilyāt - pracārasaṁvedanācca -

cittasya - paraśarīrāveśaḥ

III-39 उदानजयात् - जल - पङ्क - कण्टकादिषु -

असङ्गः - उत्क्रान्तिश्च ।

udānajayāt - jala - panka - kaṇṭakādiṣu -

asaṅgaḥ - utkrāntiśca

III-40 समानजयात् - ज्वलनम् ।

samānajayāt - jvalanam

III-41 श्रोत्राकाशयोः - संबन्धसंयमात् - दिव्यं श्रोत्रम् ।

śrotrākāśayoḥ - saṁbandhasaṁyamāt - divyaṁ śrotram

III-42 कायाकाशयोः - संबन्धसंयमात् - लघुतूलसमापत्तेश्च - आकाशगमनम् ।

kāyākāśayoḥ - saṁbandhasaṁyamāt -
laghutūlasamāpatteśca - ākāśagamanam

III-43 बहिरकल्पितावृत्तिः - महाविदेहा - ततः - प्रकाशावरणक्षयः ।

bahirakalpitāvṛttiḥ - mahāvidehā - tataḥ -
prakāśāvaraṇakṣayaḥ

III-44 स्थूल - स्वरूप - सूक्ष्म - अन्वय - अर्थवत्त्वसंयमात् - भूतजयः ।

sthūla - svarūpa - sūkṣma - anvaya -
arthavattvasaṁyamāt - bhūtajayaḥ

III-45 ततोऽणिमादिप्रादुर्भावः - कायसंपत् -
तद्धर्मानभिघातश्च ।

tato'ṇimādiprādurbhāvaḥ - kāyasaṁpat -
taddharmānabhighātaśca

III-46 रूप - लावण्य - बल - वज्रसंहननत्वानि -
कायसंपत् ।

rūpa - lāvaṇya - bala - vajrasaṁhananatvāni -
kāyasaṁpat

III-47 ग्रहण - स्वरूप - अस्मिता - अन्वय -
अर्थवत्त्वसंयमात् - इन्द्रियजयः ।

grahaṇa - svarūpa - asmitā - anvaya -
arthavattvasaṁyamāt - indriyajayaḥ

III-48 ततो मनोजवित्वं - विकरणभावः - प्रधानजयश्च ।

tato manojavitvaṁ - vikaraṇabhāvaḥ - pradhānajayaśca

III-49 सत्त्वपुरुष - अन्यताख्यातिमात्रस्य -

सर्वभावाधिष्ठातृत्वं - सर्वज्ञातृत्वं च ।

sattvapuruṣa - anyatākhyātimātrasya -

sarvabhāvādhiṣṭhātṛtvaṁ - sarvajñātṛtvaṁ ca

III-50 तद्वैराग्यादपि - दोषबीजक्षये - कैवल्यम् ।

tadvairāgyādapi - doṣabījakṣaye - kaivalyam

III-51 स्थान्युपनिमन्त्रणे - सङ्गस्मयाकरणं -

पुनरनिष्टप्रसङ्गात् ।

sthānyupanimantraṇe - saṅgasmayākaraṇaṁ -

punaraniṣṭaprasaṅgāt

III-52 क्षणतत्क्रमयोः - संयमात् - विवेकजं - ज्ञानम् ।

kṣaṇatatkramayoḥ - saṁyamāt - vivekajaṁ - jñānam

III-53 जातिलक्षणदेशैः - अन्यता - अनवच्छेदात् -

तुल्ययोः - ततः - प्रतिपत्तिः ।

jātilakṣaṇadeśaiḥ - anyatā - anavacchedāt -

tulyayoḥ - tataḥ - pratipattiḥ

III-54 तारकं - सर्वविषयं - सर्वथाविषयं - अक्रमं

चेति - विवेकजं ज्ञानम् ।

tārakaṁ - sarvaviṣayaṁ - sarvathāviṣayaṁ -

akramaṁ - ceti - vivekajaṁ jñānam

III-55 सत्त्वपुरुषयोः - शुद्धिसाम्ये - कैवल्यम् ।

sattvapuruṣayoḥ - śuddhisāmye - kaivalyam

कैवल्यपादः
Kaivalyapādaḥ

IV-1 जन्म - ओषधि - मन्त्र - तपः - समाधिजाः - सिद्धयः ।

janma - oṣadhi - mantra - tapaḥ - samādhijāḥ - siddhayaḥ

IV-2 जात्यन्तरपरिणामः - प्रकृत्यापूरात् ।

jātyantarapariṇāmaḥ - prakṛtyāpūrāt

IV-3 निमित्तमप्रयोजकं - प्रकृतीनां - वरणभेदस्तु - ततः - ततः - क्षेत्रिकवत् ।

nimittamaprayojakaṁ - prakṛtīnāṁ - varaṇabhedastu - tataḥ - kṣetrikavat

IV-4 निर्माणचित्तानि - अस्मितामात्रात् ।

nirmāṇacittāni - asmitāmātrāt

IV-5 प्रवृत्तिभेदे प्रयोजकं - चित्तमेकमनेकेषाम् ।

pravṛttibhede prayojakaṁ - cittamekamanekeṣām

IV-6 तत्र - ध्यानजम् - अनाशयम् ।

tatra - dhyānajam - anāśayam

IV-7 कर्माशुक्लाकृष्णं - योगिनः - त्रिविधमितरेषाम् ।

karmāśuklākṛṣṇaṁ - yoginaḥ - trividhamitareṣām

IV-8 ततः - तद्विपाकानुगुणानामेव - अभिव्यक्तिः -
वासनानाम् ।

tataḥ - tadvipākānuguṇānāmeva - abhivyaktiḥ -
vāsanānām

IV-9 जाति - देश - काल - व्यवहितानामपि -
आनन्तर्यं - स्मृतिसंस्कारयोः - एकरूपत्वात् ।

jati - deśa - kāla - vyavahitānāmapi - ānantaryaṁ -
smṛtisaṁskārayoḥ - ekarūpatvāt

IV-10 तासाम् - अनादित्वं - चाऽऽशिषो - नित्यत्वात्

tāsām - anāditvaṁ - cā"śiṣo - nityatvāt

IV-11 हेतु - फल - आश्रय - आलम्बनैः -

संगृहीतत्वात् - एषामभावे - तदभावः ।

hetu - phala - āśraya - ālambanaiḥ -

saṁgṛhītatvāt - eṣāmabhāve - tadabhāvaḥ

IV-12 अतीतानागतं - स्वरूपतः - अस्ति -

अध्वभेदाद्धर्माणाम् ।

atītānāgataṁ - svarūpataḥ - asti -

adhvabhedāddharmāṇām

IV-13 ते व्यक्तसूक्ष्माः - गुणात्मानः ।

te vyaktasūkṣmāḥ - guṇātmānaḥ

IV-14 परिणामैकत्वात् - वस्तुतत्त्वम् ।

pariṇāmaikatvāt - vastutattvam

IV-15 वस्तुसाम्ये - चित्तभेदात् - तयोर्विभक्तः पन्थाः ।

vastusāmye - cittabhedāt - tayorvibhaktaḥ panthāḥ

IV-16 न चैकचित्ततन्त्रं चेद्वस्तु - तदप्रमाणकं -

तदा किं स्यात् ।

na caikacittatantraṁ cedvastu - tadapramāṇakaṁ -

tadā kiṁ syāt

IV-17 तदुपरागापेक्षित्वात् - चित्तस्य - वस्तुज्ञाताज्ञातम् ।

taduparāgāpekṣitvāt - cittasya - vastujñātājñātam

IV-18 सदा ज्ञाताः - चित्तवृत्तयः - तत्प्रभोः पुरुषस्य -

अपरिणामित्वात् ।

sadā jñātāḥ - cittavṛttayaḥ - tatprabhoḥ puruṣasya -

apariṇāmitvāt

IV-19 न तत्स्वाभासं - दृश्यत्वात् ।

na tatsvābhāsaṁ - dṛśyatvāt

IV-20 एकसमये च - उभयानवधारणम् ।

ekasamaye ca - ubhayānavadhāraṇam

IV-21 चित्तान्तरदृश्ये - बुद्धिबुद्धेः - अतिप्रसङ्गः -

स्मृतिसंकरश्च ।

cittāntaradṛśye - buddhibuddheḥ - atiprasaṅgaḥ -

smṛtisaṁkaraśca

IV-22 चितेः - अप्रतिसंक्रमायाः - तदाकारापत्तौ -

स्वबुद्धिसंवेदनम् ।

citeḥ - apratisaṁkramāyāḥ - tadākārāpattau -

svabuddhisaṁvedanam

IV-23 द्रष्टृदृश्योपरक्तं - चित्तं सर्वार्थम् ।

draṣṭṛdṛśyoparaktaṁ - cittaṁ sarvārtham

IV-24 तदसंख्येयवासनाभिः - चित्रमपि - परार्थं -

संहत्यकारित्वात् ।

tadasaṁkhyeyavāsanābhiḥ - citramapi - parārthaṁ -

saṁhatyakāritvāt

IV-25 विशेषदर्शिनः - आत्मभावभावना - निवृत्तिः ।

viśeṣadarśinaḥ - ātmabhāvabhāvanā - nivṛttiḥ

IV-26 तदा - विवेकनिम्नं - कैवल्यप्राग्भारं - चित्तम् ।

tadā - vivekanimnaṁ - kaivalyaprāgbhāraṁ - cittam

IV-27 तच्छिद्रेषु - प्रत्ययान्तराणि - संस्कारेभ्यः ।

tacchidreṣu - pratyayāntarāṇi - saṁskārebhyaḥ

IV-28 हानमेषां - क्लेशवदुक्तम् ।

hānameṣāṁ - kleśavaduktam

IV-29 प्रसंख्यानेऽप्यकुसीदस्य - सर्वथा

विवेकख्यातेः - धर्ममेघः समाधिः ।

prasaṁkhyāne'pyakusīdasya - sarvathā

vivekakhyāteḥ - dharmameghaḥ samādhiḥ

IV-30 ततः - क्लेशकर्मनिवृत्तिः ।

tataḥ - kleśakarmanivṛttiḥ

IV-31 तदा - सर्वावरणमलापेतस्य - ज्ञानस्य - आनन्त्यात् - ज्ञेयमल्पम् ।

tadā - sarvāvaraṇamalāpetasya - jñānasya - ānantyāt - jñeyamalpam .

IV-32 ततः - कृतार्थानां - परिणामक्रमसमाप्तिर्गुणानाम् ।

tataḥ - kṛtārthānāṁ - pariṇāmakramasamāptirguṇānām

IV-33 क्षणप्रतियोगी - परिणामापरान्त - निर्ग्राह्यः क्रमः ।

kṣaṇapratiyogī - pariṇāmāparānta - nirgrāhyaḥ kramaḥ

IV-34 पुरुषार्थशून्यानां - गुणानां प्रतिप्रसवः - कैवल्यं - स्वरूपप्रतिष्ठा - वा - चितिशक्तिरिति ।

puruṣārthaśūnyānāṁ - guṇānāṁ pratiprasavaḥ - kaivalyaṁ - svarūpapratiṣṭhā - vā - citiśaktiriti

Part - III

Words Index

Words Index

This index lists all the Sanskrit words that occur in the *Yoga Sūtra-s* of *Patañjali*. Alongside each word is indicated the respective *Sūtra(s)* in which the word is found. For the sake of convenience, this index is presented, not in the order of occurrence of the words, but in alphabetical order. It is hoped that the reader will find this index a useful tool to identify and locate any specific word and the corresponding *Sūtra(s)* in which it appears.

A

abhāva	I-10
abhāvaḥ	I-29, II-25, IV-11
abhāvāt	II-25
abhāve	IV-11
abhibhava	III-9
abhijātasya	I-41
abhimata	I-39
abhiniveśāḥ	II-3
abhiniveśaḥ	II-9
abhivyaktiḥ	IV-8
ābhyantara	II-50, II-51
abhyāsa	I-12, I-18
abhyāsaḥ	I-13, I-32
ādarā	I-14
ādarśa	III-36
adhigamaḥ	I-29
ādhimātrāḥ	II-34
adhimātratvāt	I-22
adhiṣṭhātṛtvam	III-49

adhva	IV-12
adhyāsāt	III-17
adhyātma	I-47
ādi	III-45
ādiṣu	III-23, III-39
adṛṣṭa	II-12
āgamāḥ	I-7
ahiṁsā	II-30, II-35
aikāgrya	II-41
ajñāna	II-34
ajñātam	IV-17
akalpitā	III-43
ākāra	IV-22
akaraṇaṁ	III-51
ākāśa	III-42
ākāśayoḥ	III-41, III-42
akliṣṭāḥ	I-5
akramaṁ	III-54
akṛṣṇaṁ	IV-7
ākṣepī	II-51
akusīdasya	IV-29
alabdhabhūmikatva	I-30
ālambanā	I-10
ālambanaiḥ	IV-11
ālambanaṁ	I-38
ālasya	I-30
aliṅga	I-45
aliṅgāni	II-19
āloka	III-25

antarāyāḥ I-30
antardhānam III-21
anubhūta I-11
anugamāt I-17
anuguṇānām IV-8
anukāraḥ II-54
anumāna I-7, I-49
anumoditāḥ II-34
anupaśyaḥ II-20
anupātī I-9, III-14
anuśāsanam I-1
anuśayī II-7, II-8
ānuśravika I-15
anuṣṭhānāt II-28
anuttamaḥ II-42
anvaya III-44, III-47
anvayaḥ III-9
anya I-49, I-50, II-22
anyaḥ I-18
anyatā III-49, III-53
anyatvaṁ III-15
anyatve III-15
aparāmṛṣṭaḥ I-24
aparānta IV-33
aparāntajñānam III-22
aparigraha II-39
aparigrahāḥ II-30
apariṇāmitvāt IV-18
āpattau IV-22

āśiṣaḥ IV-10
asmitā I-17, II-3, II-6, III-47, IV-4
āśraya IV-11
āśrayatvam II-36
aṣṭau II-29
asteya II-30, II-37
asti IV-12
aśuci II-5
aśuddhi II-28, II-43
aśukla IV-7
āsvāda III-36
asya I-40
atadrūpa I-8
atha I-1
atiprasaṅgaḥ IV-21
atīta III-16, IV-12
ātma II-5, II-41, IV-25
ātmā II-21
ātmakaṁ II-18
ātmānaḥ IV-13
atyanta III-35
āvaraṇa III-43, IV-31
āvarṇam II-52
avasthā III-13
avasthānam I-3
āveśaḥ III-38
avidyā II-3, II-4, II-5, II-24
aviplavā II-26
avirati I-30

doṣa III-50
draṣṭā II-20
draṣṭṛ II-17, IV-23
draṣṭuḥ I-3
dṛḍhabhūmiḥ I-14
dṛg II-6
dṛśeḥ II-25
dṛśimātraḥ II-20
dṛṣṭa I-15, II-12
dṛṣṭaḥ II-50
dṛśya IV-23
dṛsyam II-18
dṛśyasya II-21
dṛśyatvāt IV-19
dṛśyayoḥ II-17
dṛśye IV-21
duḥkha I-31, I-33, II-5, II-8, II-16, II-34
duḥkhaiḥ II-15
duḥkḥam II-15
dvaṅdva II-48
dveṣa II-3
dveṣah II-8

E

eka I-32, IV-16, IV-20
ekāgratā III-12
ekāgratayoḥ III-11
ekam IV-5
ekarūpatvāt IV-9
ekatānatā III-2

heya II-17
heyāḥ II-10, II-11
heyaṁ II-16
hiṁsādayāḥ II-34
hlāda II-14
hṛdaye III-34

I

indriya II-18, II-41, II-43, III-47
indriyāṇāṁ II-54
indriyāṇām II-55
indriyeṣu III-13
iṣṭa II-44
īśvara I-23
īśvaraḥ I-24
īśvarapraṇidhānāni II-1, II-32
īśvarapraṇidhānāt II-45
itaratra I-4
itareṣām I-20, IV-7
itaretara III-17
iti II-34, III-54, IV-34
iva I-43, II-6, II-54, III-3

J

jala III-39
janma II-12, II-39, IV-1
japaḥ I-28
jāti II-13, II-31, III-18, III-53, IV-2, IV-9

karaṇāt	III-18
kārita	II-34
karma	I-24,II-12, III-22, IV-7, IV-30
karuṇā	I-33
kathaṁtā	II-39
kāya	II-43, III-21, III-29, III-42, III-45, III-46
khyāteḥ	I-16, II-28
khyāti	III-49
khyātiḥ	II-5, II-26
kiṁ	IV-16
kleśa	I-24,II-2, II-12, IV-30
kleśāḥ	II-3
kleśavat	IV-28
kliṣṭā	I-5
krama	III-15, IV-32,
kramaḥ	IV-33
kramayoḥ	III-52
kriyā	II-18, , II-36
kriyāyogaḥ	II-1
krodha	II-34
kṛta	II-34, IV-32
kṛtārthaṁ	II-22
kṣaṇa	III-9, III-52, IV-33
kṣaya	III-11
kṣayaḥ	III-43
kṣayāt	II-43
kṣaye	II-28, III-50
kṣetram	II-4
kṣetrikavat	IV-3

S

saṁbodhaḥ	II-39
saṁhananatvāni	III-46
saṁhatyakāritvāt	IV-24
saṁjñā	I-15
saṁkhyābhiḥ	II-50
saṁpat	III-45, III-46
saṁprajñātaḥ	I-17
saṁprayogaḥ	II-44
saṁśaya	I-30
saṁskāra	I-18, II-15, III-18
saṁskāraḥ	I-50
saṁskārāt	III-10
saṁskārayoḥ	III-9, IV-9
saṁskārebhyaḥ	IV-27
saṁtoṣa	II-32
saṁtoṣat	II-42
saṁvedanam	IV-22
saṁvedanāt	III-38
saṁvegānām	I-21
saṁvit	III-34
saṁyamaḥ	III-4
saṁyamāt	III-16, III-17, III-21, III-22, III-26, III-35, III-41, III-42, III-44, III-47, III-52
sāmye	III-55, IV-15
saṁyoga	II-25
saṁyogaḥ	II-17, II-23
saṅga	III-51
saṅgṛhītatvāt	IV-11
saṅkaraḥ	III-17, IV-21

tadapi	III-8
tadartha	II-21
tadeva	III-3
tajjaḥ	I-50
tamovṛttiḥ	I-10
tannirodhaḥ	I-12
tantraṁ	IV-16
tanu	II-4
tanūkaraṇa	II-2
tāpa	II-15
tapaḥ	II-1, II-32, IV-1
tapasaḥ	II-43
tārā	III-27
tārakaṁ	III-54
tāsām	IV-10
tasmin	II-49
tasya	I- 27, II-24, II-27, III-6, III-10, III-20
tasyāpi	I-51
tat	I-16, I-32, II-35, III-5, III-17, III-20, III-22, III-52, IV-18, IV-19, IV-27
tataḥ	I-22, I-29, II-48, II-52, II-55, III-12, III-36, III-43, III-45, III-48, III-53, IV-3, IV-8, IV-30, IV-32
tatra	I-13, I-25, I-42, I-48, III-2, IV-6
tatstha	I-41
tattva	I-32
tattvam	IV-14
tayoḥ	IV-15
te	I-30, II-10, II-14, III-37, IV-13

U

V

vivekajaṁ III-52, III-54
vivekakhyāteḥ IV-29
vivekinaḥ II-15
vratam II-31
vṛttayaḥ I-5, II-11, IV-18
vṛtteḥ I-41
vṛtti I-2, I-4, II-15
vṛttiḥ II-50, III-43
vyādhi I-30
vyākhyātā I-44
vyākhyātāḥ III-13
vyakta IV-13
vyavahita III-25
vyavahitānām IV-9
vyūha III-27, III-29
vyutthāna III-9
vyutthāne III-37

Y

yama II-29
yamāḥ II-30
yathā I-39
yatnaḥ I-13
yoga I-1, II-28
yogaḥ I-2
yoginaḥ IV-7
yogyatā II-53
yogyatvāni II-41

T Krishnamacharya

Born in 1888, Tirumalai Krishnamacharya is regarded as the grandfather of modern Yoga. Today his teachings have become very popular through his students, especially TKV Desikachar, BKS Iyengar, Pattabhi Jois and Indira Devi.

T Krishnamacharya, a direct descendant of Nathamuni, a ninth century yogi, began his formal education at the age of six, at the Parakala Math in Mysore. His thirst for knowledge inspired him to travel widely and learn all aspects of the Vedic tradition from the best teachers across India. Thanks to his perseverance and eagerness he mastered all the philosophical schools of Indian learning, Ayurveda, and Sanskrit. At the age of twenty-eight, he trekked to lake Manasarovar at the foot of Mt. Kailash, in the Himalayas, to learn Yoga from Ram Mohana Brahmachari. He left Manasarovar seven and a half years later at the command of his Guru, to share his wisdom with and for the benefit of the society at large.

Being a master of several disciplines, Krishnamacharya was offered high scholastic positions in great institutes of learning and in the courts of kings, but he chose to be a teacher of Yoga, in order to honor the promise he made to his Guru.

On many occasions he demonstrated to the world the great potentials of Yoga, in different areas of health and self control. His ability to stop his heart beat for over two minutes, using yogic practices, was indeed a notable example. With his vast learning in Yoga and other systems of Indian Philosophy, he emphasized that the practice of Yoga must be adapted to the individuals, and not the individual to Yoga. This was probably one of his most significant contributions in the field of health and healing, through Yoga.

Through his teachings, T Krishnamacharya always insisted on utilizing the spirit of Yoga to enhance the quality of our lives. He never insisted on one particular technique, but rather emphasized that techniques must be evolved to suit the needs of the individuals at the given moment. This is indeed the Yoga of Yoga. Krishnamacharya lived for over a hundred years and continued to teach till the last few days of his mortal life.

T K V Desikachar

Son and student of the great Yoga master T Krishnamacharya, TKV Desikachar is now one of the world's leading authorities on Yoga. Starting his career as an engineer, he was inspired by the teachings of his father and became his student in the 1960's. He remained his student for over thirty years until T Krishnamacharya's death in 1989.

Teaching regularly both within and outside the country, TKV Desikachar, has participated in many international conventions and conferences. He has authored numerous books and contributed to many magazines and newspapers all over the world.

His books include "Health, Healing and Beyond" and "The Heart of Yoga- Developing a Personal Practice". He has authored the first ever translation of the classical yoga text "Yogayajnavalkya Samhita". He has also co-authored with his son Kausthub, a book titled "Vedic Chant Companion". His latest work,"The Viniyoga of Yoga", co-authored by Kausthub and Frans Moors, deals with the application of asana and pranayama to suit various needs.

Krishnamacharya Yoga Mandiram

The Krishnamacharya Yoga Mandiram is a non-profit institute founded by T K V Desikachar, in 1976, to spread the teachings of the greatest Yoga master of the last century, T Krishnamacharya.

The core of T Krishnamacharya's teachings aims at integrating ancient wisdom into our modern day life situations, by respecting both the past as well as the present. It is this ability to adapt that keeps his teachings and the teachings of ancient India relevant and appropriate in our modern day living. The KYM is involved in transmitting this spirit of Krishnamacharya's teachings through Yoga classes, healing through Yoga, Yoga education and other such programs.

For more information on the KYM and its activities, please visit our website www.kym.org or ask for our brochure.